QUICK QUILTS
TO MAKE IN A WEEKEND

Rosemary Wilkinson, Editor

Henry Holt and Company
New York

Henry Holt and Company, Inc.
Publishers since 1866
115 West 18th Street
New York, New York 10011

Henry Holt ® is a registered trademark
of Henry Holt and Company, Inc.

Published in Canada by Fitzhenry & Whiteside Ltd.,
195 Allstate Parkway, Markham, Ontario L3R 4T8.

Library of Congress Catalog Card Number: 95 - 80343

ISBN 0-8050-4682-8
ISBN 0-8050-4683-6 (An Owl Book: pbk)

Henry Holt books are available for special promotions and premiums.
For details contact: Director, Special Markets.

Originally published in Great Britain in 1996
by New Holland (Publishers) Ltd.
First published in the United States in 1996
by Henry Holt and Company, Inc.

First American Edition – 1996

Created and produced by Rosemary Wilkinson Publishing, London
Art editor: Frances de Rees
Illustrator: Carol Hill
Photographer: Marie-Louise Avery
Copy editor: Michèle Clarke

Printed in Malaysia
All first editions are printed on acid-free paper.

3 5 7 9 10 8 6 4 2
1 3 5 7 9 10 8 6 4 2(pbk.)

Contents

Quick Quilt Techniques

DEVELOPMENT OF TECHNIQUES

The art of quiltmaking has been with us for many generations. Quiltmaking techniques were first brought to British shores by the crusaders who found the technique much in use in the Middle East. By the time of the Victorian era it was an established art form in many households. It was at this time that the skilled needlewoman demonstrated that she was indeed an artist and a designer, piecing together intricate designs from an array of wonderful fabrics. Much of the patchwork done at this time was either the rich 'Crazy Patchwork' in sumptuous fabrics, embellished with stitches and beads, or geometric piecing, simple geometric shapes sewn over papers before being joined together with a whipping stitch. This latter method has come to be known as 'English Paper Piecing'.

In America the pioneer women developed a technique that has become an American art form, the 'Patchwork Block'; this enables quiltmakers to piece their quilts in small units before assembling the quilt top. The revival of patchwork in Britain in the 1970s was very much based on these blockmaking techniques.

If we look at many patchwork quilt patterns they can be broken down into smaller units consisting of strips, squares and triangles. For decades these shapes have been cut using templates and pieced either by hand or machine. Such templates have been an invaluable tool for the patchworker, and indeed still are when more intricate shapes are used. However, modern lifestyles often demand a quicker approach. The advent of the rotary cutter has enabled the process to be speeded up, allowing the quiltmaker to achieve pleasing results in a much shorter time scale, for example in just a weekend. All the quilts in this book are quick projects in which the pieces are cut with a rotary cutter and machine pieced. They allow the reader to be creative in the time available, however short.

QUILT SIZES

A favourite and versatile quilt size is between 54 in and 60 in/135 cm and 155 cm square, which can be used for a baby - as a wrap, a play-rug, cot quilt and even for a while as a single bed quilt - or for an adult as a lap quilt. Larger square quilts can be used as throws. The book also features two generously sized cot quilts and a number of single bed quilts.

FABRICS
Selection

Selecting fabric for a project is a personal thing. Each of the projects included is made in the maker's own choice and it is clear to see that quiltmakers develop a unique style and taste. In each of the five sections suggestions have been given for different colourways for one of the quilts. Some of these quilts have an old-fashioned scrappy look; others have the clarity and togetherness of a planned colour arrangement.

Your fabric choice will stamp your individuality on the project. It is never possible to recreate a quilt exactly as fabric designs and colourways are always changing. To achieve interest in your quilt you need to use different tonal values and if you are using print fabrics, the scale of the print is also an important factor. The tonal values of fabric in your quilt should include light, medium and dark fabrics. These values are relative to each other so one

Equipment for the quick quilter: a quilter's rule and a plain ruler; two bias squares; a set square; a rotary cutter and mat; a red value finder; various marking pencils and quilting threads and a selection of fat quarters.

person's medium may be another person's light; the fabrics can even play different roles in the same quilt. If you are unsure of the value of the fabrics you can view them through a value finder, a red screen that eliminates the colour and allows you to see the lightness and darkness, i.e. the value. A similar effect can be achieved by photocopying fabric and looking at the value of the greyness. Another technique that you can employ is to stare at the fabric selection and gradually squint at it: the darker fabrics 'disappear' first. This is a good technique when perhaps you are confused between brightness and lightness.

The scale of the design of a print fabric is very important. Try to use a variety of scales - small prints when viewed from the distance will look like solids. Your quilt needs to hold interest both close to and from a distance. Geometric designs add movement, encouraging the eye to move over the surface and allowing you to see the other fabrics. There are also fabrics on the market now that are self-coloured prints or textured solids which are good substitutes for a solid fabric, giving a softer overall finished look.

You can always experiment with colouring a quilt design before making your fabric selection, but remember no coloured pencil or felt tip pen can recreate a single fabric or its effect when placed next to another. If you are unsure of your fabric selection purchase only a small amount and try a fabric mock-up. Quiltmakers are avid collectors of fabric, often buying without a project in mind. These fabrics can be used for some of the projects in this book; if, however, you plan to purchase additional fabrics, do take them along with you to see them together. It is very difficult to carry an image of colour in your head and finally, always be prepared to change your mind.

All the fabric sizes in this book give a margin for error, so that you can purchase fabric with confidence. Most rotary cutting projects involve the cutting of strips first; these are best cut from across the width of fabric. Therefore, take care if a design calls for a quarter: most quilting supply shops sell quarters either 'fat' or 'long'. A long quarter is cut 9 in/25 cm deep by the width of the bolt. A fat quarter is cut 18 in/50 cm deep by the width of the bolt, then split at the fold to give a piece 18 x 22 in/50 x 56 cm. Only buy a fat quarter if the design specifies such a size.

PREPARATION

All the fabric for your project must be washed separately to ensure that all excess dye is removed before working with it. Detergents of any kind are not required but the water needs to be hot. Keep rinsing until the water runs clear, this may take several rinses. This process can be done in the bath or a bowl. If you wish to use the washing machine and have no means of collecting the waste water to check for dye, place a white piece of cloth in the machine together with the fabric, if dye bleeds, it will do so into the white cloth. The process needs to be repeated until no more dye runs. If dye continues to run after repeated washes you may feel that you have to abandon this piece. It is not advisable to try setting the dye with salt or vinegar at this stage as it will only set it until the next wash and if you intend to wash your quilt, the colour will run throughout the rest of the quilt.

After washing, partially dry, then iron the fabric while still damp to replace its original crispness. Press with the selvages together just as it came off the bolt.

ROTARY CUTTING
Equipment

There are lots of different pieces of rotary cutting equipment on the market. You will need the following basic set for the quilts in this book:

Rotary cutter. These come in different sizes: small, medium and large. A good size to have is the medium, which is classed as heavy duty. The small one is good for trimming and for cutting curves. The large one is excellent for cutting large multiple layers but if you are a newcomer to the techniques, this is slightly more difficult to control. Cutters come with a safety cover which should be engaged at all times when you are not cutting. Safe habits prevent accidents from happening. Replacement blades are readily available. Keep your cutter well maintained: blunt blades will ruin your board as well as making cutting difficult and unpleasant.

Self-healing rotary cutting mat. This is essential. Do not cut on any other surface. The mats come in a variety of sizes: a good size is one on which the fabric will fit with only one fold. The boards come with a grid on one side. This grid is roller printed and is not always accurate, so do not rely on it for measurements. To avoid confusion you could always use the reverse side of the board.

Acrylic ruler. This should be a purpose-made ruler with a non bevelled edge. Never use metal rulers, as they will ruin your blades. Markings should be on the underside of the ruler and should be laser printed and easy to read. Beware of any ruler with the markings on the top surface; this leads to a parallax view of the measurements. Any angles marked on the ruler should be marked in both directions. A good size to have is 6 x 24 in/15 x 60 cm.

Bias square. This special tool will aid the cutting and squaring up of half square triangle units. A good size to have is 6 x 6 in/15 x 15 cm.

Set square. This is for straightening up the fabric. A second rotary cutting ruler will substitute for this.

All this equipment is available with either imperial or metric measurements.

MEASUREMENTS

Throughout this book all measurements are given in both imperial and metric. Fabric allowances are interchangeable for the purpose of buying the required fabric. However, all cutting instructions are not interchangeable. Use either imperial or metric: do not mix the two.

The seam allowances throughout this book (unless otherwise stated) are $\frac{1}{4}$ in if you are working in imperial or 0.75 cm if you are working in metric. You will all be aware that 0.75 cm is bigger than $\frac{1}{4}$ in, but these seam allowances work well with the rotary cutting equipment now available and are internationally accepted measurements.

All cutting instructions in this book already include seam allowances, therefore you will not need to add any extra. However, if you wish to adapt any of the quilts or create your own designs, it is worth remembering the following:

Imperial
seam allowance: $\frac{1}{4}$ in
cutting strips/squares/rectangles: add $\frac{1}{2}$ in
cutting half square triangles: add $\frac{7}{8}$ in
cutting quarter square triangles: add $1\frac{1}{4}$ in

Metric
seam allowance: 0.75 cm
cutting strips/squares/rectangles: add 1.5 cm
cutting half square triangles: add 2.5 cm
cutting quarter square triangles: add 3.5 cm

The illustrations below will show how the additions are calculated for the two types of triangles (diagram 1).

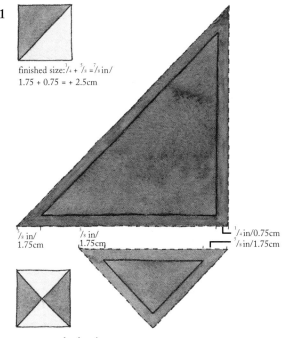

1

finished size: $\frac{1}{4} + \frac{5}{8} = \frac{7}{8}$ in/
1.75 + 0.75 = + 2.5cm

$\frac{5}{8}$ in/
1.75cm

$\frac{5}{8}$ in/
1.75cm

$\frac{1}{4}$ in/0.75cm

$\frac{5}{8}$ in/1.75cm

finished size: $\frac{5}{8} + \frac{5}{8} = 1\frac{1}{4}$ in/1.75 + 1.75 = + 3.5cm

Creating a straight edge

Regardless of how well the fabric was originally cut you will have to straighten the edge before cutting pieces for your quilt.

1 Place your fabric on the cutting board with the fold towards you and the selvage away from you and all the surplus fabric to the side in the direction of the hand you cut with.

2 Lay a set square on the fold of the fabric and line your ruler up against the square with a horizontal line on the ruler in line with the bottom of the square (diagram 2).

2

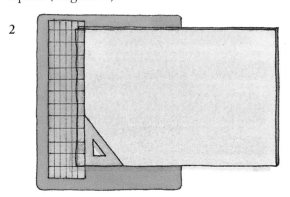

3 Place your hand at the bottom of the ruler and, starting cutting in front of the fold in the fabric, cut until your cutter is level with the top of your hand, then maintaining the pressure on the cutter, creep your hand further up the ruler, cut again and repeat the process until you have finished cutting the waste strip off (diagram 3).

3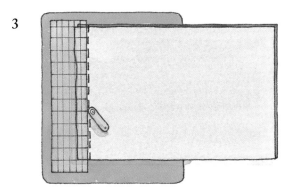

Cutting strips

1 Fold the fabric in half, so that the fold lies on top of the selvage and the cut edges lie together (diagram 4).

4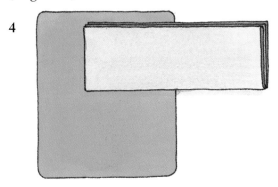

2 Place the ruler on your fabric with a horizontal line on the fold and the desired width measurement on the straightened edge. Place your hand firmly in the centre of the ruler, start cutting before the fold and cut across the fabric in one movement (diagram 5).

5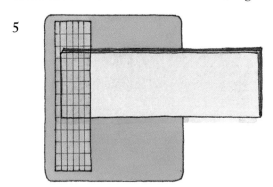

Repeat until you have cut the number of strips needed. If it becomes difficult to line up the horizontal on the fold and the measurement along the whole cut edge, repeat the straightening.

Cutting squares

1 Cut strips to the desired width.

2 Pick up the fabric with the double fold in your cutting hand and turn until it is horizontal on the board. Straighten up the end with the single fold and selvage (diagram 6).

6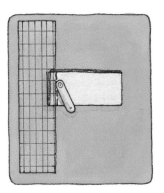

3 Using the same measurement as the initial strip, cut into squares, making sure a horizontal line on the ruler is on the bottom edge of the fabric (diagram 7). This is called subcutting.

7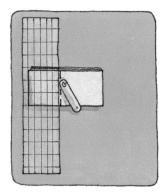

Cutting rectangles

1 Cut strips to the width of one of the measurements of the rectangle.

2 Turn the strip for cutting again, straighten the end and cut using the second measurement of the rectangle.

Cutting measurements wider than the ruler

A second ruler or square can be used to aid the cutting of wider strips (diagram 8).

8
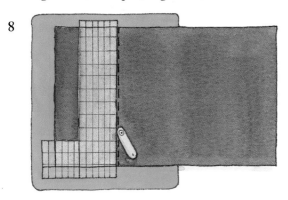

Cutting half square triangles

1 Cut strips to the desired measurement, including the seam allowances.

2 Turn for cutting again, straighten the end and cut a square.

3 Pivot the ruler until it lies exactly across the diagonal of the square. Cut into triangles (diagram 9).

9
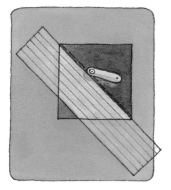

4 Repeat until you have the necessary number.

Cutting quarter square triangles

1 Cut strips to the desired measurement, including the seam allowances.

2 Turn for cutting again, straighten the end and cut a square.

3 Pivot the ruler until it lies exactly across one diagonal and cut.

4 Without moving the pieces, pivot the ruler the other way until it lies across the other diagonal and cut (diagram 10).

10

5 Repeat until you have the necessary number.

Cutting sewn strips

1 Lay the strips across the board with the surplus length towards the hand you cut with.

2 This time when trimming or subcutting, lay a horizontal line of the ruler along a seam instead of along the lower edge.

MACHINING
Setting up the machine for sewing

Start each quilt with a new needle. If you will be subcutting sewn strips, the stitch length needs to be shorter than for normal sewing. A guide is to sew at 12 stitches to the inch/5 stitches to the centimetre.

For an accurate quilt top, the seam allowance that you stitch must also be accurate, you cannot just trust in the width of your presser foot. To ensure an accurate width, work as follows:

1 Take a piece of graph paper either marked in quarter inches or in millimetres and cut the right hand edge of the paper so that you have a line exactly $\frac{1}{4}$ in/0.75 cm from the edge.

2 Place this paper under the presser foot and sew with the stitches on the line.

3 Stick a piece of masking tape on the bed of your machine along the edge of the paper. (Alternatively there are magnetic sewing guides that you can place up against the edge of the paper.)

4 Remove the paper and you are ready to stitch. It is always advisable to stitch a test piece first. Cut three short pieces of fabric 1½ in/4.5 cm wide. Sew the three strips together butting the fabric against your stitching guide. Press the seams away from the centre strip, then measure between the seam lines on the right side. If you are accurate, this measurement will be 1 in/3 cm. If it is in any way out, set up your guide again and re-test.

MACHINE PIECING

Machine piecing always appears to use an endless supply of thread, so before starting a project fill several bobbins in readiness.

Chain-piecing is a method that speeds up the whole process: stitch two pieces together, leave them under the presser foot, then butt up the next pair. Continue stitching and butting up the following pairs until you have stitched all the pieces (diagram 11).

A third piece can be added to these two in the same way (diagram 12) and the process can be repeated as often as you like. Snip the pieces apart when you have finished.

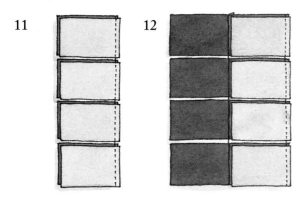

When machine piecing, the meeting of seams can, if tackled wrongly, become too bulky. Pressing instructions are given with individual projects; following these will ensure that the seams nest neatly together.

Nestling seams are where two seams that meet are pressed in the opposite direction and will then just lock together, making a neat join. It is important to match seams very carefully for accurate and attractive results.

Pressing is an important part of machine piecing, it must be done as you go along, not be left to the end, as is often the case with hand piecing.

Seams can be finger pressed first, this is when the seam is pushed over and squeezed between your thumb and finger. The work can then be pressed with an iron both on the wrong and the right side to ensure that no pleats are pressed in. Always press in the direction of the grain and not across the bias which will stretch the pieces.

ADDING BORDERS
Borders with butted edges

These borders are the easiest, and if this is your first quilt they are probably preferable. Although many of the projects in the book give measurements for the borders, always check the measurements of your quilt top before cutting these long strips.

1 To determine the length of the side borders, measure centre top to centre bottom of the quilt. Cut two borders of this length by the required width.

2 Pin and stitch to the side edges using an exact ¼ in/0.75 cm seam allowance. Press the seam towards the border.

3 Once the side borders have been stitched, measure the work again, this time from centre side to centre side. This determines the length of the top and bottom borders. Cut two border strips this length.

4 Pin and stitch to the top and bottom edges of the quilt. Press towards the border. If more than one border is required, simply repeat the process.

Borders with mitred corners

These borders take a bit more time but give a professional finish to your quilt.

1 Determine the length and width of your quilt top by measuring centre top to centre bottom and centre side to centre side.

2 Cut border pieces to these measurements plus twice the width of the border plus approximately 2 in/5 cm extra for the seam allowance.

3 Pin a border strip to the quilt edge, matching the strip centre to the quilt edge centre. Allow the excess border fabric to extend beyond each end.

4 Stitch to the quilt edge using an exact ¼ in/ 0.75 cm seam allowance, starting and finishing ¼ in/0.75 cm from the corner (diagram 13).

13

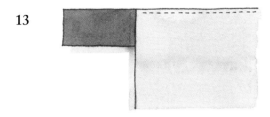

5 Repeat with remaining borders. Press the seam allowances towards the borders.

6 To form the mitres, lay the quilt wrong side up, then either press the borders as shown (diagram 14) match the folds, pin and stitch, finishing at the inner corner, or overlap the corners (diagram 15) and place the 45° line of your ruler on the raw edge of the border. Draw a pencil line from the border seam to the outside edge. Overlap the adjacent border and repeat the marking.

14   **15**

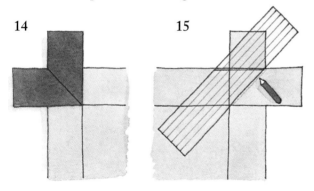

7 With right sides together, match the drawn lines, pin and stitch along the marked line (diagram 16).

16

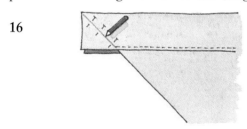

8 Check the right side, then trim to ¼ in/0.75 cm. Press this seam allowance open. Whichever method you choose, repeat on the remaining three corners.

PREPARING TO QUILT
Marking quilting designs

The marking of designs, other than the following of seam lines, should be done before the quilt is layered. Designs can be as complicated or as simple as you wish. If you intend to machine quilt, look for designs that can be stitched in a continuous motion.

There are a variety of marking tools available: 2H pencils, silver and yellow quilters' pencils, washable marking pens, etc. Whichever you choose, always test the marker on a scrap of the fabric you have used in your quilt, you should be able to remove your designs after you have quilted.

Bagging out

This is a quick method to neaten the edges of a quilt instead of adding a binding.

1 Lay the wadding out. Lay the backing fabric on top of the wadding, right side up, then lay the quilt top, right side down, on top.

2 Trim the backing fabric and the wadding to the same size as the quilt top. Take care not to cut into the quilt top when doing this.

3 Pin the layers together, then stitch round the edge of the quilt leaving a gap long enough to turn the quilt through (diagram 17).

17

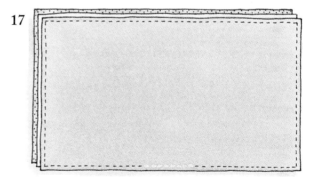

4 Trim the wadding close to the seam line, then turn the quilt through so that the wadding is in the centre of the sandwich.

5 Close the opening with small invisible ladder stitches.

6 Baste with thread or safety pins as described below.

Layering a quilt
The backing and wadding should be slightly bigger than the quilt top.

1 Lay out the backing fabric right side down, smooth out and stretch taut. If possible, stick the edge at intervals with masking tape. Lay the wadding on the top of the backing and the quilt top on the top of the wadding with right side up.

2 Pin the layers together starting from the centre and working out.

Basting
This can be done with thread or safety pins.

1 When using thread, take long pieces of thread, start in the middle and baste out to the edge in rows in both directions (diagram 18).

18

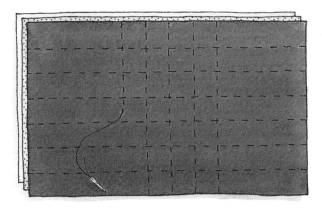

2 When using safety pins, these should be placed all over the quilt at intervals no greater than a hand's width in any one direction. Use short, fine and rustless pins to avoid marking the quilt.

3 Short plastic tags are now available that can be shot through the quilt with a basting gun instead of using safety pins.

QUILTING
The primary function of the quilting stitches is to hold the three layers of the quilt together securely enough to last the lifetime of the quilt. Hand quilting can be a slow process, therefore on the quilts featured in this book the quilting is either by machine or there are suggestions for quick hand quilting designs. You can always change from machine to hand quilting if time is not a factor.

Machine quilting
When a quilt is machine quilted, a continuous line of thread is visible on both the top and the back of the quilt; you need, therefore, to choose a lightweight thread to work with. Threads are numbered in such a way that the lighter the thread, the higher the number. Before quilting your project, make up a sample sandwich of backing, wadding and top fabrics as used in the quilt and try different threads to achieve the effect that you like. You can even choose an invisible thread if you wish.

Needles are numbered 70/10, 80/12, 90/14, etc. The finer the needle, the lower the number: 70/10 or 80/12 are suitable for both piecing and quilting with lightweight or invisible thread.

A walking or even-feed foot is essential to prevent tucks forming in the quilt top or backing. This foot is used with the feed dogs up and therefore is the best technique for designs with continuous, fairly straight lines. You can turn wide curves and pivot but you cannot turn tight curves. It is used for stitching in-the-ditch, simple outline stitching and stitching in a grid design. For tight curves or freehand quilting, you will need to use the darning foot with the feed dogs down.

When you are using a walking foot, the machine controls the direction and the stitch length. In general, the stitch length needs to be longer than for regular sewing. To start and end a line of quilting, set the stitch length to very short and sew about 8 stitches, then snip off the loose threads close to the surface of the quilt.

In-the-ditch
One of the simplest, and therefore most popular, methods of machine quilting is quilting in-the-ditch. When a top is pieced and pressed all the seams have a low side with no seam allowance underneath: this is the ditch. The quilting is done on this side close to the seam.

Freehand quilting

With this method you control the direction and the length of the stitches by moving the quilt forwards, backwards and sideways under the needle. You will need much practice to achieve perfect results.

Hand quilting

To hand quilt you need to select a stronger thread than that used for normal sewing. There are several makes of quilting thread on the market. Choose a colour of quilting thread that will either blend or contrast with the fabrics, the choice is yours. If you wish, you can use different colours in the same quilt. Special needles called 'betweens' are used and you need to select a 9, 10 or 12. The larger the number, the smaller the needle. The quilt top needs to be held flat in either a hoop or a frame.

Frame

Some floor frames do not require the quilt to be basted; the layers are held together by the frame.

1 Tack the backing fabric, wrong side up, to the tape that is fixed to the front and back rollers of the frame. Roll the excess backing fabric onto the back roller until the fabric in the frame is taut.

2 Attach the bottom edge of the wadding to the backing fabric along the front roller only, using long basting stitches. Smooth the wadding towards the back of the frame.

3 Arrange the quilt top over the wadding; baste through all three layers along the front edge only.

4 To hold the wadding and quilt top in position along the far edge of the frame, use long, fine pins or needles. The wadding and quilt top hang loose over the back roller.

5 Quilt the area in front of you, then release the tension and roll more backing off the back roller. Wind the quilted part onto the front roller, re-tension and continue to quilt.

Hoop

Hoops can be hand-held (round and oval) or on a floor stand. If you are using a hand-held hoop choose a 14 in/35 cm or 16 in/40 cm diameter for ease. Hoops on floor stands can have a bigger diameter. Hoops are considered to be more portable and they allow you to turn the work. Do not leave a quilt in a hoop when you are not working on it, as this will distort your piece.

Layer and baste the quilt with thread as described opposite, then place the quilt over the bottom ring and place the top ring over the quilt. Tighten the ring: the fabric need not be as tight as a drum skin, but the work should be smooth. Work from the centre outwards.

Simple scroll frames are also available which will allow you the portability of a hoop while working with a frame.

The quilting process

The goal in hand quilting is to form straight, even stitches with the same size space in between as the length of thread showing.

1 Cut a length of thread about 18 in/45 cm long and tie a single knot in the end cut from the spool.

2 To start quilting, enter the work with a flat knot about ¾ in/2 cm from where you want to start quilting, run the needle through the wadding only and come up at the starting point. Pull the thread sharply and the knot will 'pop' through the surface and lodge in the wadding.

3 To quilt, the needle needs to enter the fabric at a perpendicular angle. Hold the needle between your thumb and forefinger and place the point where you wish to form the first stitch. Push the needle through the quilt, so that it only just pierces the under surface, then lodge the eye of the needle in the end of your thimble. The end of your forefinger under the quilt will just feel the tip of the needle. Some quilters like to wear a second thimble or some other protection on the finger of their underneath hand.

4 The underfinger pushes upwards at the same time as the thimble rocks the eye end of the needle towards the surface of the quilt. The point of the needle will reappear through the top.

5 Rock the needle with the thimble into a perpendicular position and re-enter the fabric.

6 Repeat until you have a few stitches on the needle.

Pull the thread through and repeat the process (diagram 19).

19

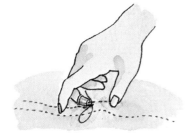

7 To finish off, quilt until you have about 6 in/ 15 cm of thread left, then make a knot by passing the needle round the thread to form a loop and passing the needle through the loop. Pull the loop to the surface of the quilt and tighten to form a knot. Take one more stitch and 'pop' the knot through the surface. Take the needle through the wadding and back through the surface of the quilt, pull the thread taut, then cut close to the surface.

TYING A QUILT

A quick alternative to quilting is tying. The thread for this needs to be thicker; cotton perlé is good. A sharp needle with a large eye is essential. Use a long length of thread to allow for multiple tying.

1 Starting in the centre of the place where you wish to position the tie, take a stitch through all three layers, draw the thread through, leaving a tail about 6 in/15 cm. Re-enter the quilt at the point where the next tie is to be and take another stitch.

2 Repeat, without cutting, until there is a stitch in each of the places to have a tie (diagram 20).

20

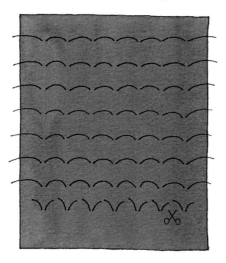

3 Cut between the stitches, then tie the threads using a surgeon's square knot (diagram 21).

21

BINDING THE QUILT

After quilting, trim the edges, so that all three layers are level. The binding is best done with doublefold binding which can either be cut straight or on the bias.

Continuous strip bias binding

1 Cut a square and mark the edges A, B, C and D; cut through the diagonal (diagram 22), then stitch A to B with a ¼ in/0.75 cm seam allowance (diagram 23).

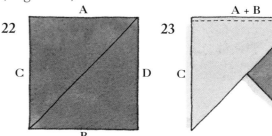

2 Open out and press the seam open. Draw lines the width of the bias you are making on the wrong side of the fabric (diagram 24).

24

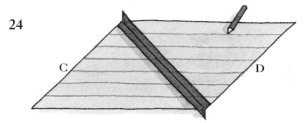

3 Make a tube by joining C to D, right sides together, but dropping the seam by one strip and match the marked lines. Pin and stitch the seam (diagram 25). Press open.

25

4 Cut the tube open along the lines in a continuous line (diagram 26).

26

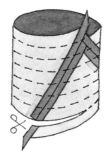

Doublefold binding

1 Fold the bias in half lengthwise, right side out, and press lightly.

2 Starting somewhere along one edge of the quilt, start to pin the binding to the quilt, leaving a tail (diagram 27).

27

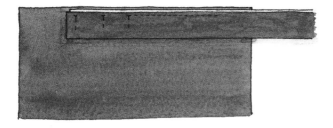

3 Stitch, using ¼ in/0.75 cm seam allowance, until you are ¼ in/0.75 cm from the corner. Reverse stitch and break off the thread.

4 Fold the binding away from the quilt at a right angle (diagram 28), then fold it back down on itself, matching the edge of the binding with the edge of the quilt (diagram 29).

28

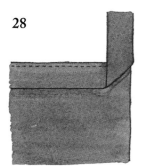

29

5 Starting ¼ in/0.75 cm from the corner, stitch to the next corner and repeat. Continue in this way until you are back where you started.

6 To finish, fold back the two ends (diagram 30). Finger press and stitch the binding together along the creases. Trim back to ¼ in/0.75 cm.

30

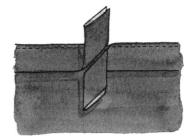

7 Turn the binding over the edge to the back of the quilt, slip stitch down covering the machine stitches. At the corners, mitres will fall on both front and back.

LABELLING A QUILT

It is important to sign and date your quilt. The label you stitch onto your quilt can be simple or elaborate. There are books of scrolls that you can trace onto a simple calico label with a fine permanent pen. You can iron freezer paper to the wrong side of the label and type the details on the fabric. Remove the freezer paper before stitching the label to the reverse of the quilt.

ADDING A HANGING SLEEVE

If your quilt is to be hung, either on the wall at home or in an exhibition, it will need a hanging sleeve.

1 Cut a piece of fabric 9 in/23 cm wide and as long as the quilt is wide. Turn a ½ in/1 cm hem at each end and machine stitch.

2 Fold in half along its length, right sides together, and stitch the raw edges together with a ½ in/1 cm seam. Turn right sides out and press, so that the seam is in the middle.

3 Slipstitch the sleeve to the back of the quilt along the top and bottom edges, placing the top edge just below the binding and making sure that the seam side is underneath.

Quick Country Quilts

GILL TURLEY

On my travels I have seen and admired many antique quilts. I have a particular affection for the old quilts in Sweden and these have influenced the designs for both the Country Comforter and the Feedsack Scrap quilts. The woollen fabrics brought back memories of Amish and Welsh quilts, while the indigo blues instantly transported my thoughts to the Far East. All the quilts in this chapter have been designed with a country look and above all they are intended for everyday use.

For speed and accuracy most pieces will be rotary cut. Buttons, ties and utility quilting have been used to complete the quilts. I have used a natural cotton wadding throughout. This needs to be washed before use, though the manufacturers are now producing a similar type that comes ready-washed. This wadding does not need to be closely quilted: the rows of quilting can be spaced up to 10 in/25 cm apart.

Cinnamon & Navy Wool Throw

THIS SIMPLE 'SQUARE WITHIN A SQUARE' design is often found in the old Welsh and Amish quilts. Although the Amish often made quilts from woollens, as a rule they would not have used any patterned fabrics. The lightweight woollen fabrics used here give a soft rural feel to the quilt and they come in wider widths which can be used to advantage. The quilt could be used on a bed or as a throw.

Quilt size: 61½ x 61½ in/156 x 156 cm

MATERIALS

All fabrics are lightweight wool 60 in/152 cm wide
Checked fabric for borders and four of the centre squares: 1 yard/1 metre
Dark plain fabric for four corner squares and five of the centre squares: ½ yard/50 cm
Medium plain fabric background: ¾ yard/70 cm
Backing: 65 x 65 in/165 x 165 cm
Wadding (cotton or wool): 65 x 65 in/ 165 x 165 cm
Extra strong thread in contrasting colour for quilting
Binding: 29 x 29 in/74 x 74 cm

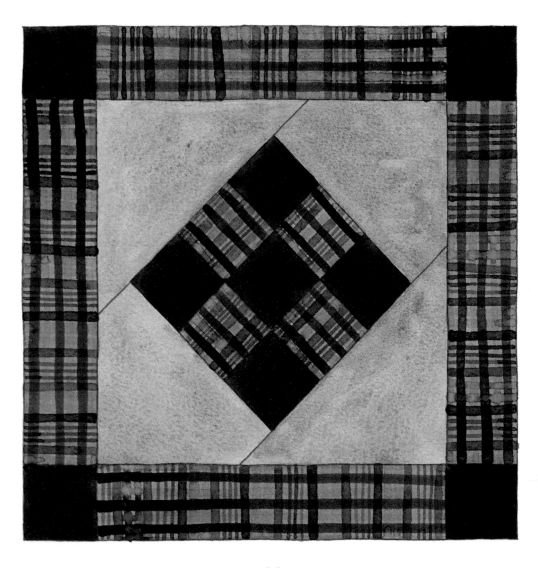

A quite different effect is achieved by using crisp cottons instead of the soft woollen fabrics: a combination of pink and cream fabrics is crisp and summery; plain and striped fabrics in subdued greens are brought to life by the sprigged floral print; earth tones are given added warmth with a rich, red centre square and blue and green checks of different scales produce a fresh, country look.

21

CUTTING

1 From the checked fabric, cut 4 strips 9 in/23 cm wide. From one end only of each of these strips cut 1 square for the quilt centre, i.e. 4 squares, 9 x 9 in/23 x 23 cm (diagram 1). The remainder of these long strips will be used for the 4 borders, put these to one side and cut them to size when the quilt has been pieced.

1

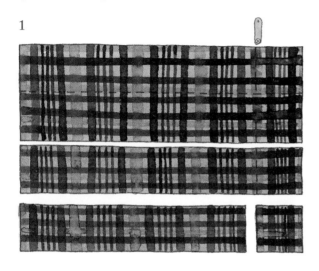

2 From the dark plain fabric, cut 9 squares: 4 for corners and 5 for centre square, 9 x 9 in/23 x 23 cm (diagram 2).

2

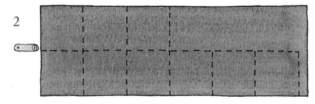

3 From the medium plain fabric, cut 2 squares, 27 x 27 in/66 x 66 cm; cut each of these on the diagonal, making 4 large triangles (diagram 3).

3

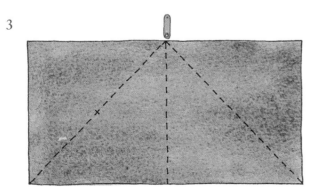

SEWING

1 Piece together the centre square: stitch five of dark plain fabric and four of checked fabric squares, placing them in the traditional nine-patch design (diagram 4).

4

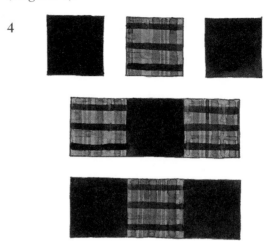

2 Pin the bias edges of the large background triangles to the edges of the centre nine-patch square, matching centres. It is advisable to work on one at a time, as follows.

3 Pin top right, large triangle to first nine-patch centre square edge and machine stitch. Press the seam towards the centre, or if fabric is bulky press the seam open. The excess triangle fabric that over-hangs the edge of the centre pieced square will need to be trimmed off. Use a long ruler and carefully check the angle before cutting (diagram 5).

5

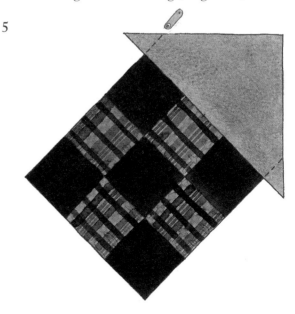

4 Pin the next triangle to the opposite edge of centre nine-patch square, matching centres, machine stitch and press. Trim excess triangle fabric as before.

5 Join the two remaining triangles edges in the same way. There will be no need to trim these two.

ADDING THE BORDERS

1 To determine the length for all four borders, measure pieced quilt from centre top to centre bottom and from centre side to centre side. The measurement should be the same in both directions. Using this measurement, cut the borders from the remaining long pieces of border fabric.

2 Stitch corner squares to each end of top and bottom borders. Press the seams, either open or towards the border.

3 Stitch side borders to the sides of the quilt. Press seams. Stitch top and bottom borders to the quilt.

FINISHING THE QUILT

1 Layer the backing, wadding and quilt top (see page 14), then quilt by hand using thick thread and a large-eyed needle. The quilt plan shows one possible design for quilting. For greater speed, the top could be machine-quilted.

2 To finish, make a bias binding 2 ½ in/6.5 cm wide, using the continuous strip method (see page 16). Fold in half lengthwise and use to bind the quilt edges taking a ¼ in/6 mm seam allowance (see page 17).

Quick Quilted Country Comforter

THIS QUILT ACHIEVES ITS COUNTRY appearance by the edge-to-edge placement of the plaids, stripes and checks. Too much time spent arranging the patches will lose the random look and make the layout appear too organized.

This is a comforter to be used and loved. Keep it on the sofa ready to protect you from winter draughts or use it to cover a sleeping child.

Quilt size: 47 x 60 in/118 x 149.5 cm

MATERIALS

Assorted plaids, checks and striped fabrics (31 different patches): 10 x 10¾ in/25.5 x 27 cm each. **Note:** If you are purchasing fabric especially for this project it would be more economical to work with just eight different fabrics and cut four patches from each, giving a total of 32 patches, one of which will be spare. In this case you will need to buy 8 x ⅓ yard/30 cm pieces of fabric, 45 in/115 cm wide.

One packet of small sticky labels
Backing: 50 x 65 in/127 x 162 cm
Wadding: 50 x 65 in/127 x 162 cm
Quilting thread: choose the thickness of thread according to the weight of the fabric you are using
Binding: 24 x 24 in/60 x 60 cm

CUTTING

If using purchased fabric, cut into rectangles each 10 x 10¾ in/25.5 x 27 cm.

SEWING

1 Using 20 of the patchwork pieces, lay them out on the floor at random. Place the short edges parallel to the top and bottom of the quilt. Quickly arrange them into five rows of four patches, until you are pleased with the layout. **Note:** two shocking colours placed next to each other will serve to lessen the shock and will work better than isolating the brightly coloured patches. Use the small sticky labels to number each patch.

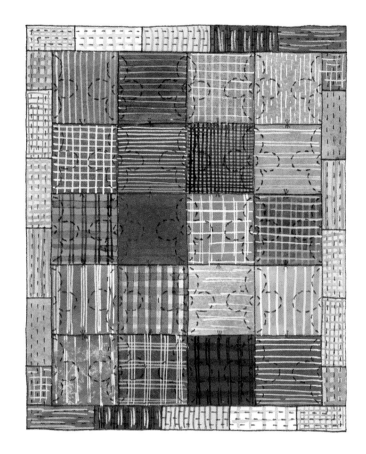

2 Following the number order, join the patches into rows, stitching long edge to long edge. Remove all labels before pressing work. Press the seams on the odd numbered rows to the left of the work and the seams on the even numbered rows to the right of the work (diagram 1).

1

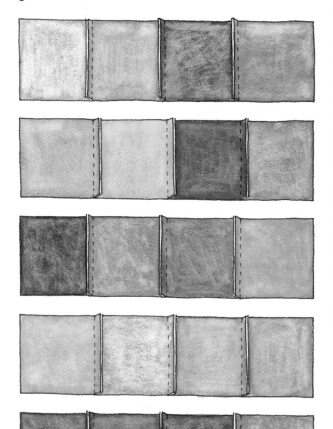

3 Stitch the rows together.

ADDING THE BORDERS

1 Take the remaining eleven patches and cut one or two in half cutting across the width of the patch. When arranging the border layout, position these half patches apart from each other. By doing this the seams on the border and centre patchwork should be staggered and will not sit directly on top of each other.

2 Join all the border patches into one long strip, seaming them together along the short edges. Press the seams together in one direction.

3 Cut the long pieced strip in half lengthwise, ready to make the borders of 5 in/12.5 cm width.

4 For the side borders, measure through the centre of the pieced quilt top, centre top to centre bottom to determine the length. Cut this measurement from the two long border strips and machine them to the quilt sides. Press seams towards the borders.

5 For the top and bottom borders, measure through the centre of the pieced quilt top, side edge (centre) to side edge (centre), to determine the length of each one. Cut these from the remaining border strips and stitch them to top and bottom edges of the quilt. Press seams towards the borders.

FINISHING THE QUILT

1 Prepare the work for quilting either in a hoop or a frame (see page 15).

2 To make the quilting template, trace the flower template (diagram 2) either directly onto template plastic or onto paper. Stick the paper onto strong card and cut out carefully, following the outline.

3 To mark the design on the quilt, position the template so that the flower is centred over the vertical seams and draw round the outline with chalk, marking each flower as you are ready to quilt that particular section. Quilt by hand (see page 15).

4 The border can be quilted with straight lines which can be marked out with masking tape as required.

5 To finish, make a bias binding 2 in/5 cm wide, using the continuous strip method (see page 16). Fold in half lengthwise and use to bind the quilt edges taking a $1/4$ in/6 mm seam allowance (see page 17).

2

Oriental Indigo & White Country Quilt

THIS QUILT WAS MADE FROM A collection of odd-sized pieces of indigo and white, batik-printed cotton. To give the quilt a rustic appearance, unbleached calico was used in preference to the bleached, white variety. The colour scheme gives the quilt a strong feel of Japan. It brings to mind their batik-printed fabrics, indigo working clothes, and above all the clear, uncluttered approach associated with Japanese design.

The instructions describe a quick method of construction using just four different blue and white fabrics and natural calico. This economical use of material will achieve a similar effect but with greater speed. The quilt could be used on a single bed or would make an attractive wallhanging.

Quilt size: 48½ x 54½ in/123.5 x 137.5 cm

MATERIALS
Unbleached calico for lattice strips, borders and quilt back: 2½ yards/2.5 metres, 50 in/127 cm wide
Four different blue and white fabrics (home-dyed, indigo or batik): ⅓ yard/30 cm of each, 45 in/115 cm wide
Wadding: 50 x 60 in/127 x 153 cm
Buttons: 80 or more
Red or blue heavy thread: for tying the quilt layers together (thread must be colourfast)
Binding (contrast colour or calico): 24 x 24 in/ 60 x 60 cm

CUTTING

1 Cut off enough calico for the quilt backing, 50 x 56 in/127 x 142 cm. From the remaining piece of calico, cutting across the width of the fabric, cut 7 lattice strips, 2½ x 42½ in/6.5 x 108.5 cm and 4 strips, 3½ x 48½ in/9 x 123.5 cm for the borders.

2 From each of the blue and white fabrics cut 1 strip, 9½ x 42½ in/24.5 x 108.5 cm.

SEWING

1 Machine stitch the four printed strips to three of the calico lattice strips, joining the long edges. Do not add outer borders at this stage (diagram 1). Press the seams on the wrong side of the work so that they face towards the printed fabrics.
Note: Strong prints may show through the calico if the seams are pressed towards the calico strips.

1

2 Cut across the width of the pieced work, cutting rows at the following intervals (diagram 2):

2

row A: 6½ in/16.5 cm
row B: 7½ in/19.5 cm
row C: 8½ in/21.5 cm
row D: 9½ in/24.5 cm
row E: 10½ in/26.5 cm

3 On your work surface, lay the rows out in alphabetical order. Turn rows B and D so that on these two rows only, fabric number four is now on the left-hand side of the work (see quilt plan).

4 Machine stitch the remaining four lattice strips to the pieced rows. Press seams towards the patterned fabrics.

ADDING THE BORDERS

1 Machine stitch side borders to the quilt. Press the seams towards the centre of the quilt.

2 Stitch the top and bottom borders to the quilt. Press the seams towards the centre of the quilt.

FINISHING THE QUILT

1 Baste the quilt layers together as described on page 14.

2 Secure the layers by stitching the buttons on the front of the quilt, using the same thread to make decorative ties on the back as described in steps 3 to 5. Buttons should be positioned in the corners of the patches; larger patches may require a fifth button in the centre.

3 Thread the needle with several strands of thread. Bring the needle through from the back of the work to the front, so that the needle arrives in the corner of the patch. Leave ends loose on the back of the work for tying.

4 Pass the needle through the holes in the button and push it through to the back of the work. (Do this twice if the holes in the buttons allow enough thread space.)

5 On the back of the work tie threads securely and leave decorative ends or tufts; these should be approximately ¾in/2 cm long.

Safety note: Never use buttons on a quilt intended for use by babies and young children. Instead it would be safer to just tie the quilt (see page 16).

6 To finish, make a binding 2 in/5 cm wide using the continuous strip technique (see page 16). Press strip in half lengthwise and use to bind the quilt (see page 17).

Provençal Ribbons

FRENCH PROVENÇAL FABRICS FROM A fabric market in Paris were chosen for this quilt. Their strong colours reflect for me the warmth of the Midi countryside. Red and green prints were used to make the zig-zag 'ribbons' and the mitred borders were cut from a yellow and multi-coloured striped print.

In summer this quilt could be taken into the garden and thrown over a hammock or bench; in winter its vibrant colouring would add warmth to a country kitchen.

Quilt size: 49½ x 56½ in/127x 145 cm

MATERIALS

Red print: 1 yard/1 metre (58 in/148 cm wide) or 1¼ yards/1.25 metres (45 in/115 cm wide)
Green print: 1 yard/1 metre (58 in/148 cm wide) or 1¼ yards/1.25 metres (45 in/115 cm wide)
Border print: 2 yards/2 metres (45 or 58 in/ 115 or 148 cm)
Backing: 60 x 60 in/153 x 153 cm
Wadding: 60 x 60 in/153 x 153 cm
Cotton perlé: for ties
Binding: 24 x 24 in/60 x 60 cm

CUTTING

1 From the wider fabric width, cut 3 red strips and 3 green strips, 8¼ in/21.5 cm, cutting across the width. Alternatively, from the narrower fabric width, cut 4 red strips and 4 green strips, 8¼ in/21.5 cm across the fabric width.

2 Cut these strips into 20 squares, 8¼ x 8¼ in/ 21.5 x 21.5 cm. Cut the squares twice across the diagonal to produce 80 quarter-square triangles per colour (78 needed in total). The long edge of this quarter-square triangle is cut on the straight grain of the fabric. This runs along the length of the quilt and will add stability (diagram 1).

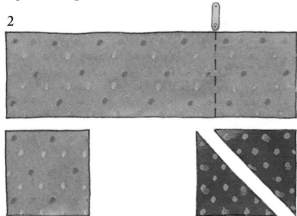

1

3 From the remaining red and green fabrics, cut 6 squares from each, 4 ³⁄₈ x 4 ³⁄₈ in/11.5 x 11.5 cm. Cut the squares once diagonally to produce 12 half-square triangles per colour (diagram 2). These are used at the ends of the rows to offset the quarter-square triangles.

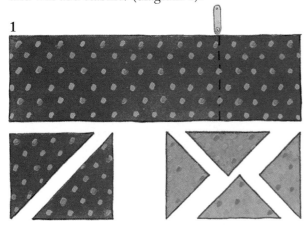

2

4 For borders, see step 1 in 'Adding the borders'.

SEWING

1 Twelve rows of pieced triangles are required for the quilt: six 'A' strips and six 'B' strips. Start each row with a half-square triangle: the long (bias) edge of this triangle is joined to the short edge of the first quarter-square triangle.

2 Alternating colours and stitching the triangles short edge to short edge, continue joining the quarter-square triangles. There will be seven of one colour and six of the other colour per row, plus two half-square triangles, one at each end. Press the seams in one direction (diagram 3).

3   B   A

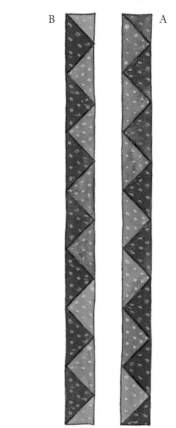

3 Join the twelve rows, seaming the long edges together. Press seams in one direction.

ADDING THE BORDERS

1 Measure through the centre of the quilt to determine the lengths for the borders. The width of the border fabric stripe will dictate the width cut for the borders. As the corners are to be mitred, at each end of each border, add the border width (in this example, 4 ¼ in/11 cm), plus a little extra fabric to give enough length for the mitres. Cut the border strips to these measurements.

2 Pin borders to quilt, matching centres. Stitch borders to all four sides of the quilt. Carefully fold and mitre the corners, checking the 45° angles before stitching (see page 12).

3 Layer the backing, wadding and quilt top and baste in a grid (see page 14).

4 Tie the quilt (see page 16), placing the ties along the seam of every second row, as shown in the quilt plan on page 32. Alternatively, you could hand quilt with 'big stitch' quilting to echo the zig-zags (see page 39); or machine-quilt along the ribbon lines.

5 To finish, make a bias binding 2 in/5 cm wide, using the continuous strip method (see page 16). Fold in half lengthwise and use to bind the quilt edges taking a ¼ in/6 mm seam allowance (see page 17).

Feedsack Scrap Quilt

The quilt shown here was made from old, feedsack fabric, from the USA. The colour scheme might have been very bland but is saved by the two brighter prints which create an accent and provide a surprise to the eye. This square quilt has a generous border which would overhang a single bed and would look very attractive on an antique bed. On a double bed it could be used as a top quilt.

These 1930s fabric sacks were used not only for feed but also for flour, sugar and salt. They were popular during the Depression years when money was short and times were hard. The sacks were made from cheap fabric, some had the brand name stamped over them and others were printed with colourful designs, in geometric and floral patterns; plain pastel colours also featured. As well as being used in quilts, feedsacks could be recycled and used for all sorts of household items.

Quilt size: 57³/₄ x 57³/₄ in/145 x 145 cm

MATERIALS
Fabrics used here are 45 in/115 cm wide.

Quilt centre fabric: a total of six pieces, each 9 x 44 in/25 x 112 cm. (Choose four assorted light and medium prints plus two accent/shock prints, or use equivalent amount of scrap fabric.)
Border fabric (plain): 1¼ yards/1.25 metres
Corner fabric (patterned): ¼ yard/25 cm
Backing: 60 x 60 in/153 x 153 cm plain or patterned cotton
Wadding: 60 x 60 in/153 x 153 cm
Extra strong thread: cotton perlé, buttonhole/carpet thread or fine crochet cotton for quilting; lighter weight fabric will require thinner thread
Binding: 24 x 24 in/60 x 60 cm contrasting fabric

CUTTING

1 Carefully layer all 6 quilt centre pieces. Cut strips 3¼ in/8.5 cm wide lengthwise. When using thicker fabrics, cut fewer layers at a time.

2 To give your quilt a random look, cut these long strips into 3 or 4 shorter ones of unequal length.

3 From the plain fabric, cut the 2 side borders 8½ x 41¾ in/21.5 x 106.5 cm. Cut the top and bottom borders after making the quilt centre.

4 From the patterned fabric, cut 4 squares, 8 ½ x 8½ in/21.5 x 21.5 cm for the border corners.

SEWING

1 Mix the quilt centre fabrics and stitch the short edges together. Continue until you have made a long strip (approximately 17 yards/16 metres).

2 On your kitchen table or work surface stick two pieces of masking tape, 41¾ in/106.5 cm apart (this marks the length for the strips for the quilt centre).

3 Using the masking tape as a guide, measure off and cut 15 strips, 3¼ x 41¾ in/8.5 x 106.5 cm, from the long fabric strip that you have just completed. Avoid starting or finishing a row with a very short strip (less than 2 in/5 cm is not advisable). If this occurs at the finishing end of the strip, shorten the long strip and add a longer piece of fabric; measure again and trim to required length (diagram 1). If this occurs at the beginning of a strip, trim off the short piece, then measure off the next length as described (diagram 2).

4 Arrange the strips side by side. Machine stitch, this time joining the long edges together (the strips will run from the top to the bottom of the quilt, see quilt plan, page 36).

5 On the wrong side of the work, press the seams together.

1

2

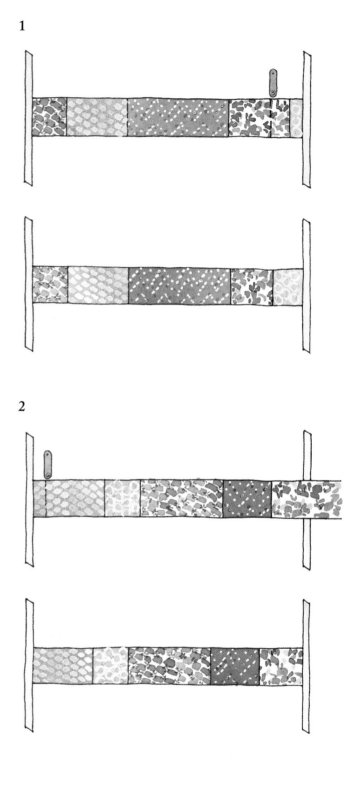

ADDING THE BORDERS

1 Machine the side borders to the side edges of the patchwork centre. Press seams together, towards the borders.

2 Before you cut the top and bottom borders, measure to double check the width of your patchwork piece, measuring from the centre of the left-hand edge to the centre of the right-hand edge. It should measure 41¾in/106.5 cm. If your seam widths are not 100% exact, this measurement will vary; if this is the case, cut your top and bottom borders so that their lengths match the width measurement of your patchwork.

3 Machine the four corner squares to each end of the top and bottom borders, taking a ¼ in/0.75 cm seam allowance. Press the seams together towards the border centre.

4 Machine the top and bottom borders to the patchwork.

FINISHING THE QUILT

1 Prepare the work for quilting either in a hoop or a frame (see page 15).

2 Mark the quilting lines as you go; there is no need to mark them all in advance (see quilt plan). Use either a ruler and chalk, or you can use masking tape as a guide line.

3 For 'big stitch' quilting you will require a needle with an eye large enough to take the heavier thread. Make evenly spaced running stitches, approximately ¼ in/0.75 cm in length. The rows do not need to be as close together as they are in traditional quilting.

4 When quilting has been completed, remove the quilt from the frame or hoop.

5 For strength, make a bias binding 2 in/5 cm wide, using the continuous strip method (see page 16). Fold in half lengthwise and use to bind the quilt edges (see page 17).

Autumn and Winter: Double-sided Log Cabin Tablecloth

These double-sided, rectangular log cabin blocks can be quickly put together in the traditional 'Straight Furrow' design to produce a tablecloth which can be used on the front or reverse side. Choose two different colour schemes: you may like to select colours suitable for different festivals, e.g. Christmas (red, white and dark green) and Easter (yellow, white and light green).

In order that the dark fabrics do not show through the light fabrics, if possible, back dark fabric with dark and light fabric with light. To ensure accuracy choose fabrics that are of the same weight: 100% dressweight cotton is recommended.

Both sides of this patchwork are stitched at the same time, as you stitch a strip to the front of the work so you also stitch one to the back. Time is saved as there is no quilting involved.

Tablecloth size: 56 x 66 in/140 x 171 cm
Total number of blocks: 25
Block size: 10 x 12 in/25 x 30 cm
Finished width of strips (in blocks): 1¼ in/3 cm
Finished width of lattice strips: 1 in/2.5 cm

MATERIALS
All fabrics are 45 in/115 cm wide.

Centre rectangles fabric (two different cottons):
⅓ yard/30 cm each
Dark and light strips (four different cottons: two dark fabrics and two light): 1¾ yards/1.75 metres of each.
Border/lattice fabric for joining the blocks together (choose a colour which will suit both sides):
2 yards/2 metres

COLOUR CHART GUIDE

Make a simple, quick colour chart to use as guide, as follows:

1 Take a sheet of paper (A4 size will do) and draw a vertical line to divide the area in half. One half represents the front of the work and the other half represents the back.

2 Cut a small sample square from each of your chosen fabrics, stick these to the relevant sections of your colour chart (use double-sided sellotape for this), decide which colour scheme will be the front of your cloth and which the back, then label the pieces accordingly:

FRONT
centre
light strip A
dark strip B
lattice/border

3 Repeat this for the back on the remaining half of the colour chart and label the pieces

BACK
centre
light strip C
dark strip D
lattice/border

CUTTING

1 To cut the centre rectangles, layer and press the two centre fabrics wrong sides together. Cut into 25 pairs of rectangles, 2½ x 4½ in/8.5 x 13.5 cm. Leave the pairs stacked together, front side up.

2 To cut the strips, fold the fabric, raw edge to raw edge, then in half again, placing folded edge to raw edges. From folded fabric, cut strips 1¾ in/ 4.5 cm wide, cutting parallel to the selvages, along the length of the fabric. Do not include the selvage in the strips as it is woven more tightly, can shrink during washing and may distort the work.
Note: The strips could be cut across the width of the fabric, but would be more likely to stretch and therefore be less accurate.

3 From the lattice fabric, cut 1½ in/4 cm strips lengthwise.

SEWING

Begin by making a sample block to learn the method and to test for accuracy. Once this has been achieved, you will be familiar with the technique and it will then be much quicker to chain-piece the blocks, working on four or more at a time. Always work from the front of the block as it helps prevent any confusion with placement of front and back fabrics. Refer to the plan for order of piecing (diagram 1).

1

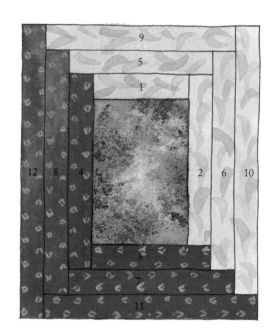

Piecing the sample block

1 Take one pair of centres, layered wrong sides together with the front fabric on top.

2 For row 1, position the first light strips on either side of one short edge of the centre pieces: A on the front, C on the back. The strips must always be placed right sides together. When you are sure all four layers are even at the edges, machine stitch through all layers, taking a ¼ in/0.75 cm seam allowance (diagram 2).

2

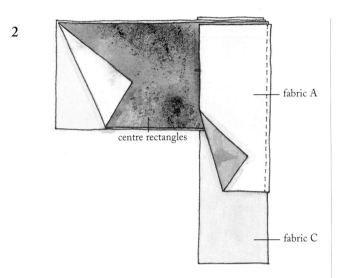

centre rectangles

— fabric A

— fabric C

3 Press seams accurately. Never attempt to press the front and the back seams at the same time. This can produce unwanted folds on the underside strips. Press seams one at a time, as follows: press the seam on front, away from the centre rectangle; turn the work over and now press the seam on the back, away from the centre.
Note: The raw edges should be even.

4 Using ruler and rotary cutter, trim away excess strip fabric, double checking measurements as you do so. The sewn-in strip should now measure 1½ in/75 cm.

5 Working in a clockwise direction, for row 2 (with row 1 at the top of the work) stitch light strips A and C to the long edge of rectangle (diagram 3). Press, double check the measurements, then trim.

3

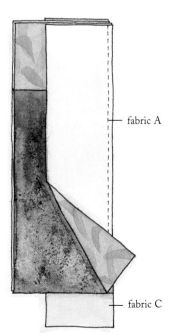

— fabric A

— fabric C

6 For row 3 (with row 2 at the top of the work), stitch the dark strips B and D to the remaining short edge (diagram 4). Press and trim.

4

fabric D

fabric B

7 For row 4 (with row 3 at the top of the work), stitch dark strips B and D to the remaining long edge (diagram 5). Press and trim.

5

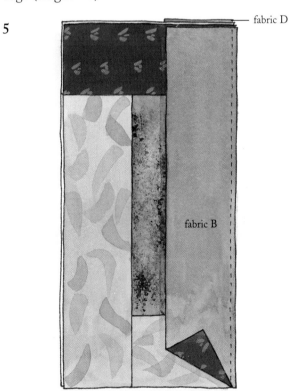

— fabric D

fabric B

8 Repeat these four rows in the same order until there are three rows of strips on each side of the rectangle. The sample block is now complete.

43

Piecing the remaining 24 blocks

1 These can be chain-pieced but it is worth remembering that this will only prove to be a quick method for stitching the blocks provided you pick up and place the fabrics in the correct position and colour order, so beware! Before you stitch, check the position of the strips on the front and back of the work. Check that the light and dark fabrics are in the correct order.

2 For row 1, take light A and C long strips as before, and machine stitch them to the short edge of the first pair of centre rectangles. Do not cut the thread at this stage. Leave the needle in the four layers of fabric, and raise the machine foot.

3 Pick up next pair of centre rectangles, lift up strip A only (the uppermost strip) and position the second pair of centre rectangles so that the short edges are parallel to long strip C underneath. Replace strip A, so that all raw edges align on the right-hand side, then stitch.

4 Continue inserting centres in this way, until you have stitched the first row strips to all the centres.

5 Press work, as described for sample block. Cut the blocks apart checking the measurements carefully as you do so.

6 For row 2, (with row 1 at the top of the work), position light A and C long strips on front and back of first piece (which now consists of centre + row 1). Stitch. Continue to slot in the units and stitch in the same way.

7 For rows 3 and 4, repeat the process on the two unstitched sides of the rectangles, using darks strips B and D. As the rows increase and the units become larger it will only be possible to fit a few blocks to each strip length.

8 Continue adding rows in this manner, until all 25 blocks are complete.

Joining the blocks with the lattice strips

1 On a flat surface, lay the blocks out in the 'Straight Furrow' arrangement (see quilt plan).

2 Join as follows: begin with the vertical lattice strips, working from top to bottom of the quilt. Keep the blocks in strict order and take the first block (number 1, top left) and two lengths of lattice strips. Place the block so that the right-hand long edge is sandwiched between the lattice strips, with the right sides of the fabric together. Machine stitch.

3 With the second block (number 6), chain-piece as before.

4 Continue until all five blocks have been stitched to the lattice (diagram 6).

6

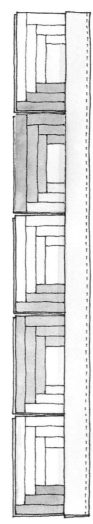

5 When this first row is complete, press the seams away from the blocks. Cut these units apart and trim if necessary, so that the edges are level. Replace the blocks in their original position according to the quilt plan. On the next row, again working from top to bottom of the quilt, place the unstitched edge of the top lattice strip over the left-hand long edge of the first block and stitch through three layers (top lattice + the two layers of the block, the back layer of lattice remaining free). Chain-piece the remaining blocks.

6 Turn under the seam allowance on this back layer of lattice and finger crease. Baste and carefully machine stitch this edge down using a zig-zag stitch. Match thread to both the top and bottom fabrics or use invisible thread on the top side. The folded edge rests on top of the previous line of stitching. Alternatively, this could be slip-stitched by hand but will of course take longer.

7 Repeat this process until all the vertical rows have been joined along the long edges with lattice strips, five rows in all.

8 Measure four lengths for horizontal strips, these should equal:

finished block width x 5
+ finished lattice width x 4
+ seam allowance x 2
= 54½ in/136.5 cm

9 Now join the horizontal rows, using the same method. Make sure that the blocks are aligned and all fabric layers are flat.

ADDING THE BORDERS

1 Measure the length for side border strips. These should equal:

finished block length x 5
+ finished lattice width x 4
+ seam allowance x 2
= 64½ in/161.5 cm

The width for these strips should be 1½ in/4 cm as before.

2 Stitch each set of border strips together, along one of the long edges, right sides together.

3 Turn work through so that fabric is right side out and press seams thoroughly.

4 To attach the borders, place the border on top of the tablecloth side, right sides together and aligning the raw edges but pin along the underneath long edge of the border only. Machine through all three layers (two layers of tablecloth plus one layer of border).

5 Turn under seam allowance on the unstitched long edge, finger-press and stitch it down as before.

6 Measure length for top and bottom border strips. These should equal:

finished block width x 5
finished lattice width x 4
finished side borders x 2
seam allowance x 2
= 56½ in/141.5 cm

The width for these strips should be 1½ in/4 cm as before.

7 With right sides together machine front to back border pieces stitching along the two short edges and one long edge. Leave the other long edge open (diagram 7). Turn the borders through so the fabric is right side out and press the seams thoroughly.

7

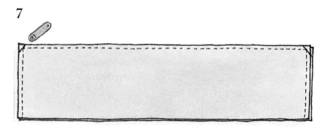

8 Pin borders to each end of tablecloth, right side of border with the fabrics right sides together, and machine stitch as for side borders (one layer of border and two layers of tablecloth).

9 On unstitched, raw edges of both borders, turn under seam allowance, finger-press, baste and stitch down as before.

Quick Strips

ANNE WALKER

Using strips and bars is one of the quickest and easiest techniques in patchwork and gives great opportunities for play and experiment with colour. It is a good introduction to rotary cutting, as there are no difficult angles involved, and gives good practice for straight neat seaming on the machine.

I have chosen four traditional patterns: two use blocks cut from strips which have already been joined, one uses long strips which are cut down as you stitch the block and the other is quickly pieced from large bars to serve as a perfect medium for quilting. The fifth quilt, the Bargello Quilt, is also made from pieced strips which are subcut but these, when joined, form the complete quilt top.

Amish Bars

THIS TRADITIONAL QUILT HAS BEEN made to the same design by many generations of Amish women for use in their family homes. The quilt is simple to construct as it contains so few pieces, thus allowing time to be devoted to the quilting. The Amish traditionally use solid colours to reflect their simple lifestyle. The impact of their quilts is in the juxtaposition of light and dark fabrics. This quilt is always square and holds the same proportions whatever the overall size: the seven central bars are always half the width of the outer border and twice that of the inner border. It makes a dramatic wallhanging or throw.

Quilt size: 60 x 60 in/180 x 180 cm

MATERIALS
All fabrics used in the quilt top are 45 in/115 cm wide

Black fabric: 2 yards/2 metres
Bar fabric: ½ yard/75 cm
Inner border fabric: ½ yard/75 cm
Inner border squares: ⅛ yard/10 cm
Outer border squares: ⅜ yard/40 cm
Backing and binding fabric: 3½ yards/3.8 metres
Wadding: 64 x 64 in/190 x 190 cm

These fabric collages of the quilt in miniature give a good impression of the full size effect of the juxtaposition of different colours. Black bars and borders have been used in all versions with four different solid colours in each. These are made up of light and dark tones of the same colour and an accent colour, giving an overall harmony to the quilt, so characteristic of Amish designs. Note how the light shades accentuate different parts of the design.

CUTTING

1 From the black fabric, cut 4 strips, 10½ x 40½ in/31.5 x 121.5 cm for the outer borders, and 4 strips, 5½ x 35½ in/ 16.5 x 106.5 cm, for the bars.

2 From the bar fabric, cut 3 strips, 5½ x 35½ in/16.5 x 106.5 cm.

3 From the inner border fabric, cut 4 strips, 3 x 35½ in/9 x 106.5 cm.

4 For the inner border squares, cut 4 squares, 3 x 3 in/9 x 9 cm.

5 For the outer border squares, cut 4 squares, 10½ x 10½ in/31.5 x 31.5 cm.

6 Cut the backing fabric in half and join to make a rectangle, 64 x 90 in/190 x 230 cm. From this rectangle, cut a square 64 x 64 in/190 x 190 cm.

7 For the binding, cut strips 2¼ in/6 cm wide.

SEWING

1 Lay out the seven pieces for the centre right side up in the order: black - bar - black - bar - black - bar - black.

2 Flip the bar fabric onto the black strip to the left and stitch in pairs with an exact ¼ in/0.75 cm seam allowance; chain-piece until you have three pairs of strips.

3 Snip apart and join these three stitched pieces together ensuring that the colours alternate.

4 Add the single black strip to the right-hand edge to complete the central section.

ADDING THE BORDERS

1 Add a strip of inner border to each of the side edges, and press all seams towards the black strip (diagram 1).

1

2 Join an inner border square to each end of the two remaining inner border strips and press towards the squares.

3 Pin and stitch these strips to the top and bottom of the quilt top, taking care to match the seams where appropriate, and press towards the border (diagram 2)

2

4 Join an outer border strip to each of the side edges, and press towards the border (diagram 3).

3

4

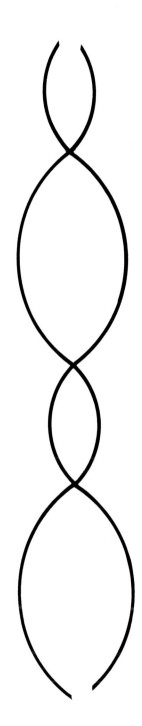

a

5 Join an outer border square to each end of the two remaining outer border strips, and press towards the border.

6 Join these pieces to the top and bottom of the quilt top and press towards the border.

FINISHING THE QUILT

1 The quilt top is now ready to mark with quilting lines. Simple ideas have been included (diagrams 4a, b, c and d). These patterns were used on the quilt in the photograph but you could mark with designs of your own choice for quilting by hand or machine.

2 Layer the backing, wadding and quilt top. Pin, then baste the layers in a grid.

3 Quilt by hand or machine as desired.

4 When the quilting is complete, stitch the binding strips together as required and use to bind the quilt with a doublefold binding (see page 17).

b

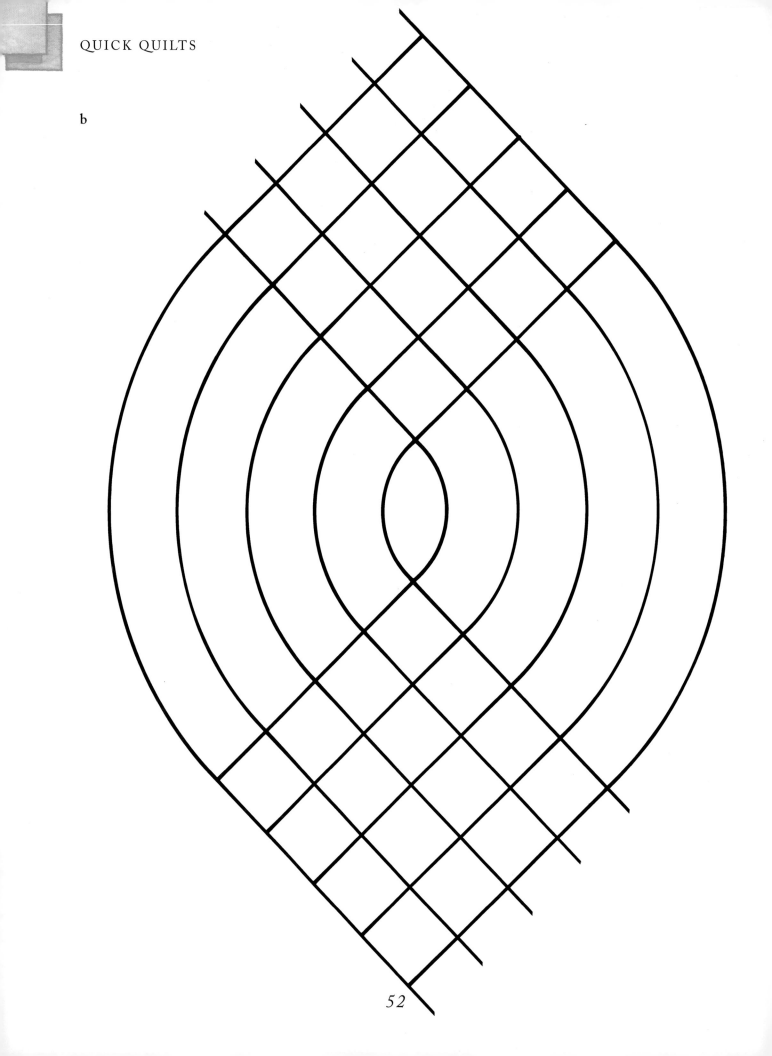

c

d

Triple Rail Fence

THE 'TRIPLE RAIL FENCE' IS ONE OF THE simplest blocks to make. It is cut from units of three pieced strips. This is an excellent quilt to make both to familiarize yourself with your rotary cutting equipment and to practise piecing on the machine. This would make a cosy lap quilt or an attractive top quilt for a single bed.

Quilt size: 48 x 57 in/130 x 150 cm

MATERIALS

All fabrics used in the quilt top are 45 in/115 cm wide

Light fabric: ¾ yard/75 cm
Dark A fabric: ½ yard/50 cm
Dark B fabric: ½ yard/50 cm
Dark C fabric: ½ yard/50 cm
Medium fabric: ½ yard/50 cm
Inner border/backing and binding fabric: 3 yards/3 metres
Wadding: 50 x 60 in/140 x 165 cm

CUTTING

1 From the light fabric, cut 13 strips, 2 in/5.5 cm wide.

2 From each of the dark and medium fabrics, cut 8 strips, 2 in/5.5 cm wide.

3 Cut your inner border/backing and binding fabric in half and join to form a rectangle, 54 x 90 in/150 x 230 cm. Press the seam open.

4 From this cut a rectangle, 50 x 60 in/ 140 x 165 cm and reserve for the backing.

5 From the remainder, cut 4 strips, 2 x 54 in/ 5 x 137 cm; cut 1 strip, 5 in/13.5 cm wide and from this cut 4 squares, 5 x 5 in/13.5 x 13.5 cm, and finally cut the rest into 2¹⁄₂ in/6 cm strips for the binding.

SEWING

Two slightly different blocks are combined to form this quilt, set 1 and set 2 (diagram 1).

1

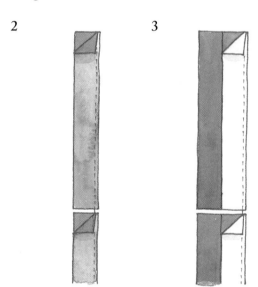

set 1   set 2

Set 1

1 Lay out five sets of strips right side up in the order: dark A - dark B - light.

2 Flip B onto A, right sides together, and stitch with an accurate ¹⁄₄ in/0.75 cm seam. Chain-piece all the As to the Bs. Do not cut the threads (diagram 2).

3 Open out the As and Bs, and chain-piece the light strip to each of the Bs in the same manner (diagram 3).

2   3

4 Cut the joining threads and press the seams to the darkest side of the unit, then press both on the right and the wrong side to ensure that no folds or wrinkles appear.

5 Measure across these units in the middle of the strip from raw edge to raw edge.

6 Using the measurement, cut your units into squares; you will need 40.

Set 2

1 Lay out five sets of strips in the order: light - medium - dark C.

2 Stitch into five units as before.

3 Press, measure and cut into squares. Again you will need 40.

CONSTRUCTION OF THE QUILT TOP

1 Lay out the blocks as shown in the quilt plan.

2 Stitch the blocks together to form rows across the quilt, pressing towards the vertical blocks.

3 When all 10 rows are stitched, join the horizontal seams, matching the appropriate seams. Press all these seams one way.

ADDING THE BORDERS

1 Measure the width of your top from centre side to centre side. Use this measurement to cut two border strips, then add to the top and bottom edge, pinning from the centre out. Stitch. Press towards the border fabric.

2 Measure the length of your top from centre top to centre bottom. Using the two remaining border strips, add a border of the correct length to the side edges, pinning from the centre out. Stitch. Press towards the border fabric.

3 Stitch the remaining strips from your block fabrics in random units of 5 strips.

4 Press the seams in one direction and cut into 5 in/13.5 cm pieces. Join these strips to make two borders with 26 small strips and two borders with 32 small strips. Remove any extra pieces where necessary. Press all seams one way.

5 Pin one of the longer border strips from the centre out to each of the side edges. Stitch with an accurate ¼ in/0.75 cm seam. Press towards the inner border.

6 Stitch a 5 in/13.5 cm square to each end of the shorter border pieces. Press towards the squares (diagram 4).

4

7 Pin these strips from the centre out to the top and bottom of the quilt; stitch, matching corner seams. Press towards the inner border.

FINISHING THE QUILT

1 Layer the backing rectangle, wadding and quilt top. Pin and baste in a grid pattern starting from the centre and working out (see page 14).

2 Quilt in the pattern of your choice. I have machine-quilted 'in-the-ditch' following the lines of the blocks.

3 When the quilting is complete, stitch the binding strips together as required and use to bind the quilt with a doublefold binding (see page 17).

Autumn Steps

THIS QUILT USES THE 'COURTHOUSE STEPS' variation of the very popular 'Log Cabin' block. The splashes of colour of the autumnal leaves gave the inspiration for this quilt. The colours are captured forever in this comforter to give cheer on dull grey days.

Quilt size: 56 x 56 in/120 x 120 cm

MATERIALS
All fabrics used in the quilt top are 45 in/115 cm wide

Centre square fabric: ¼ yard/30 cm
Green fabrics for the 'steps' (5 different shades): ½ yard/50 cm each
Yellow/orange fabrics for the 'steps' (5 different shades): ½ yard/50 cm each
Backing and border fabric: 3 ½ yards/3.5 metres
Binding fabric: ½ yard/50 cm
Wadding: 60 x 60 in/130 x 130 cm

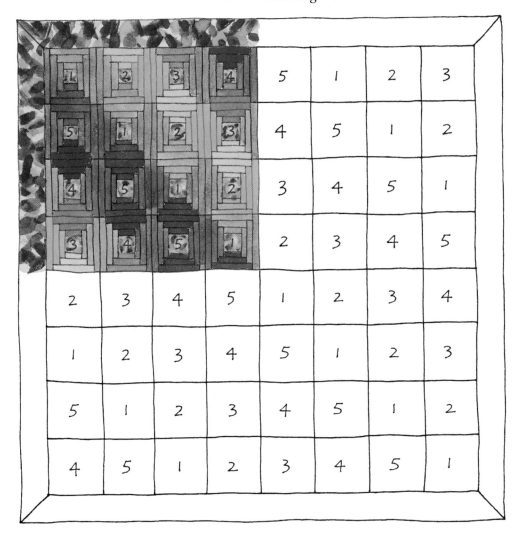

CUTTING

1 For the centre squares, cut 4 strips, 2 in/5.5 cm wide. Cut these strips into 64 squares.

2 For the 'steps', cut all the fabrics into strips, 1¼ in/3.5 cm wide.

3 For the backing and borders, cut the fabric in half and join into a rectangle, 63 x 90 in/ 140 x 230 cm. Press the seam open. Cut from this a square, 60 x 60 in/130 x 130 cm for the backing.

4 From the remainder, cut 4 strips, 4½ x 63 in/11.5 x 140 cm.

5 Cut the binding into 2¼ in/6 cm strips.

SEWING

First identify the greens as 1-5, and the yellow/oranges as A-E. There are five different blocks in this quilt, using a combination of the five greens and five yellow/oranges (diagram 1).

1

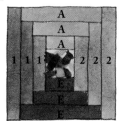
block 1 (make 14)

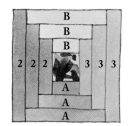
block 2 (make 13)

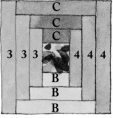
block 3 (make 12)

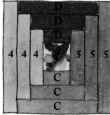
block 4 (make 12)

block 5 (make 13)

Block 1

1 Take an 'A' strip and place it under your machine foot, right side up. Take a centre square and place face down on the strip, lining up the raw edges and stitch with an accurate ¼ in/0.75 cm seam. Chain-piece the centre squares in this way until you have stitched all 14 (diagram 2). Press towards the strip and cut apart, trimming the strip length to match each square (diagram 3).

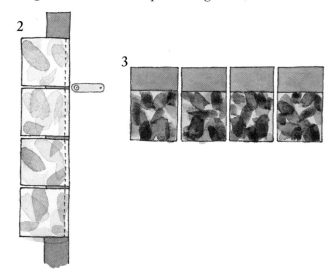

2 Take an 'E' strip and place it under the machine foot and stitch the first unit to it, right sides together, chain-piecing as before (diagram 4). Press towards the strip. Cut apart and trim.

4

3 Take a no. 1 strip and place it under the machine foot. Stitch the unit to it, right sides together, chain-piecing as before (diagram 5). Press towards the strip. Cut apart and trim.

5

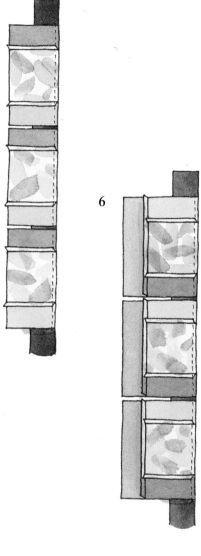

6

7

4 Take a no. 2 fabric and place it under the machine foot. Stitch the unit to it, right sides together, chain-piecing as before (diagram 6). Press towards the strip. Cut apart and trim.

5 Repeat steps 1 to 4 twice more. The block is now complete (diagram 7).

Blocks 2 to 5

Make these in the same manner, using the fabrics shown in the placement chart for each block (diagram 1). Remember to label the blocks from numbers 1 to 5.

PIECING THE QUILT TOP

1 Lay out the blocks as in the quilt plan. Stitch the blocks together in rows. Press odd rows to the left and even rows to the right.

2 Pin and stitch the horizontal rows together, taking care to match the seams at all times. Press all these seams in one direction.

ADDING THE BORDERS

1 Measure the quilt top from centre side to centre side. Find the middle of a border strip and mark with a pin. Measure the distance of half the quilt, away from this pin.

2 Match the border strip to the centre and edges of the quilt top and pin in place. Stitch in place, starting and finishing ¼ in/0.75 cm from the corners. Repeat with the other three strips.

3 Press towards the borders. Mitre the corners as described on page 12.

FINISHING THE QUILT

1 Layer the quilt top, wadding and backing. Pin and baste in a grid formation from the centre out.

2 Quilt in the pattern of your choice. I have machine-quilted diagonal lines in a grid across the quilt following the line of the 'steps'.

3 Bind with the binding strips, joined where necessary, in a doublefold binding (see page 17).

Roman Stripes

THIS IS ANOTHER SIMPLE QUILT FROM THE Amish, which again looks its best in solid colours with the dark half of the block being either black or navy to show off the other colours. Use the quilt as a throw or as a topper for a single bed.

Quilt size: 60 x 60 in/150 x 150 cm

MATERIALS
All fabrics used in the quilt top are 45 in/115 cm wide

Five different fabrics for stripes: ½ yard/50 cm each
Inner border fabric (use one of the stripe fabrics): ¾ yard/75 cm
Outer border/backing/binding fabric: 4 yards/4 metres
Dark fabric: 2 yards/2 metres
Wadding: 64 x 64 in/160 x 160 cm

CUTTING

1 For the stripes, cut 8 strips, 1¾ in/4.5 cm wide from each of the 5 fabrics.

2 For the inner border, cut 8 strips, 2½ in/6.5 cm wide.

3 From the backing fabric, cut off ½ yard/50 cm for the binding and from this cut strips, 2¼ in/6 cm wide.

4 Cut the remaining backing fabric in half and stitch together to form a rectangle, 64 x 90 in/ 160 x 230 cm. Cut from this a square, 64 x 64 in/160 x 160 cm for the backing.

5 From the remainder, cut 4 strips, 4½ x 64 in/11.5 x 160 cm for the outer borders.

SEWING

Making the striped units

There are two different blocks both made from a striped triangle and a plain dark one (diagram 1). Both are assembled in the same way.

1

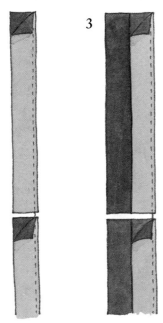

block 1   block 2

1 To make the striped half, lay out the five fabrics in stacks in the order that you want the colours to appear, the outer two fabrics will dominate so make sure you like these the most.

2 Flip the second strip, right sides down, onto the first strip, and stitch with an exact ¼ in/0.75 cm seam; chain-piece until you have stitched all the second strips to the first (diagram 2).

3 Do not cut the strips apart; open them up and place the third strip over the second, right sides together. Chain-piece the third strips (diagram 3).

2   3

4 Continue adding on the fourth and fifth strips in the same manner. Cut the threads holding the units together.

5 Press all the seams to one side, pressing on the right and the wrong side to ensure that no folds are pressed into the units.

6 On the wrong side measure the width of your finished unit from raw edge to raw edge. Measure several units in different places and take an average.

Adding the dark side

1 Using this measurement cut eight strips from your dark fabric.

2 Place a dark strip, right sides together, with a striped piece. Pin together down the outside edges. Stitch down these outside edges using an accurate ¼ in/0.75 cm seam. Stitch all eight dark strips to the eight striped units (diagram 4).

4

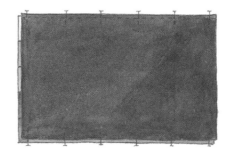

Cutting off the blocks

1 Lay one stitched piece on your cutting mat, stripes facing down. Lay a second piece on top with the colours running the opposite way (diagram 5).

5

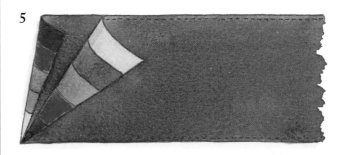

2 Place the 45° line of a 6 x 24 in/15 x 60 cm ruler on the top straight edge of the sewn pieces. Place the edge of the ruler at the right-hand edge of the strip. Cut along this edge with your rotary cutter (diagram 6).

3 Pivot the ruler and match the other 45° line on the top edge of the stitched pieces and the edge of the ruler to the tip of the last cut. Cut again (diagram 7).

6

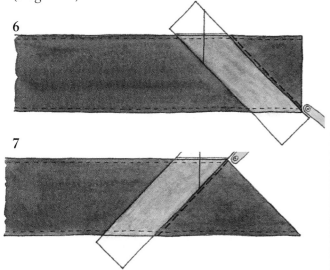

7

4 Continue pivoting your ruler, matching and cutting. You will make six cuts across the strip (diagram 8). Pair up the remaining six units in the same way and cut in the same manner.

8

5 Unpick the few stitches from the tips of the triangles. Press the seams to the dark side of the block and snip off the untidy tips.

COMPLETING THE QUILT TOP

1 Lay out the blocks in a 'Pinwheel' design as in the quilt plan.

2 Piece each row horizontally. Press odd rows to the left and even rows to the right. Stitch the rows together matching the seams where appropriate. Press all these seams one way.

ADDING THE BORDERS

1 Using the inner border strips, stitch together in pairs to make four long strips. Press seams open.

2 Measure across the centre of your quilt top. On each border strip measure half this distance from

the centre seam and place a pin.

3 Attach the borders to the quilt top as described on page 61. Mitre the corners (see page 12).

FINISHING THE QUILT

1 Layer the backing, wadding and quilt top; pin and baste in a grid, starting from the centre.

2 Quilt in the pattern of your choice. I have machine-quilted 'in-the-ditch'.

3 When the quilting is complete, stitch the binding strips together as required and use to bind the quilt with a doublefold binding (see page 17).

ALTERNATIVE SIZES

To keep the pinwheel design, the size can be increased by adding two blocks to the width and two blocks to the length. This will give a quilt measuring 90 in/230 cm, suitable for a double bed. Make 15 units as described on page 64.

Fabric requirements
Five different fabrics for stripes: 1 yard/1 m each
Inner border fabric (use one of the stripe fabrics): 1 1/8 yards/110 cm
Outer border/backing/binding: 6 1/2 yards/ 6.5 metres
Dark fabric: 4 yards/4 metres
Wadding: 95 x 95 in/240 x 240 cm

Adding three blocks to the original quilt width and three to the length will make a king size bed quilt, 104 x 104 in/270 x 270 cm. Make 20 units as described on page 64.

Fabric requirements
Five different fabrics for stripes: 1 1/4 yards/125 cm each
Inner border fabric (use one of the stripe fabrics): 1 1/3 yards/135 cm
Outer border/backing/binding: 10 yards/10 metres
Dark fabric: 5 yards/5 metres
Wadding: 110 x 110 in/280 x 280 cm

Bargello Quilt

BARGELLO QUILTS HAVE BECOME A fashionable interpretation of bargello tapestry. The construction is based on techniques first used by the Seminole Indians.

You can be as imaginative as you wish with your fabrics. Below is laid out a formula which will produce a stunning quilt for you, but once you have an idea of the technique you can create your own designs with a different selection of fabrics to produce an absolutely individual piece. This intriguing design makes a striking wallhanging.

Quilt size: 47 x 55 in/144 x 144 cm

MATERIALS

All fabrics used in the quilt top are 45 in/115 cm wide

10 different fabrics (either shaded from light to dark or two colourways shaded with an accent if desired): ½ yard/50 cm each.

Inner border fabric in accent colour (best chosen after middle section is complete): ½ yard/50 cm

Outer border/backing fabric: 3¼ yard/3.25 metres

Binding fabric (you can use accent border material): ½ yard/50 cm

Wadding: 58 x 60 in/150 x 150 cm

CUTTING

1 Cut each of the 10 fabrics across the width into 5 strips, 2 in/5.5 cm wide.

2 From the inner border fabric, cut strips, 1¼ in/3.5 cm wide.

3 Cut the outer border and backing fabric in half and join to form a rectangle, 58 x 90 in/ 150 x 230 cm. From this rectangle, cut another piece, 50 x 58 in/150 x 150 cm for the backing. From the remainder, cut 4 strips, 4½ x 58 in/ 11.5 x 150 cm.

4 From the binding fabric, cut several strips 2¼ in/6 cm wide.

SEWING

1 Lay out one strip from each of the ten fabrics in the order that you like them best.

2 Stitch in sets of ten using an accurate ¼ in/ 0.75 cm seam. Press the seams in alternate directions (diagram 1).

1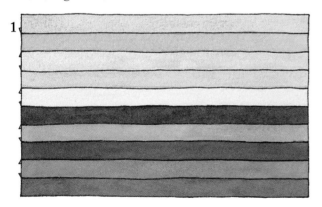

3 The stitched strips are now ready to cut at right angles to the seams. Cut the following amount:

Width of strip	Number of strips
3 in (7.5 cm)	9
2 in (5.5 cm)	27
1½ in (4 cm)	21
1⅛ in (3.5 cm)	24
⅞ in (2.5 cm)	21

4 Join three strips of the same width together end to end (diagram 2).

2

5 Continue to join the strips in the same manner until all pieces are 30 units long. Join the ends of the each strip to form a circle (diagram 3).

3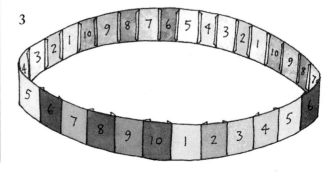

6 Next unpick the circles to form new strips, following the chart. Lay out the strips in the order given, starting from the left. The first strip will have fabric 5 at the top and fabric 4 at the bottom.

	Size of strip	Top fabric	Bottom fabric
Row 1	2 in/5.5 cm	5	4
Row 2	3 in/7.5 cm	6	5
Row 3	2 in/5.5 cm	7	6
Row 4	1½ in/4 cm	8	7
Row 5	1⅛ in/3.5 cm	9	8
Row 6	⅞ in/2.5 cm	8	7
Row 7	⅞ in/2.5 cm	7	6
Row 8	1⅛ in/3.5 cm	6	5
Row 9	1⅛ in/3.5 cm	5	4
Row 10	1⅛ in/3.5 cm	4	3
Row 11	1½ in/4 cm	3	2
Row 12	1½ in/4 cm	4	3
Row 13	1½ in/4 cm	5	4
Row 14	2 in/5.5 cm	4	3
Row 15	2 in/5.5 cm	3	2
Row 16	2 in/5.5 cm	2	1
Row 17	2 in/5.5 cm	1	10
Row 18	2 in/5.5 cm	10	9
Row 19	1⅛ in/3.5 cm	9	8
Row 20	⅞ in/2.5 cm	8	7
Row 21	1⅛ in/3.5 cm	7	6
Row 22	1½ in/4 cm	6	5
Row 23	⅞ in/2.5 cm	5	4
Row 24	3 in/7.5 cm	4	3
Row 25	1⅛ in/3.5 cm	3	2
Row 26	⅞ in/2.5 cm	2	1
Row 27	⅞ in/2.5 cm	1	10
Row 28	1½ in/4 cm	10	9
Row 29	2 in/5.5 cm	9	8
Row 30	3 in/7.5 cm	10	9
Row 31	⅞ in/2.5 cm	1	10
Row 32	1⅛ in/3.5 cm	2	1
Row 33	1½ in/4 cm	3	2
Row 34	2 in/5.5 cm	4	3

7 Join these unpicked strips in order, starting from the left and matching all horizontal seams as you go. Press in one direction.

ADDING THE BORDERS

1 Measure the length of the quilt from centre top to centre bottom and cut two inner border strips to this length. Pin these strips to the sides of the quilt top, starting from the centre and working outwards. Stitch, then press towards the border.

2 Measure the width of the quilt from centre side to centre side and cut two more inner border strips to this measurement. Pin these strips to the top and bottom from the centre out. Stitch, then press towards the border.

3 Measure the width of the quilt again through the centre. Mark the centre of the quilt at top and bottom with a pin. Mark the centre of two outer border strips and a point half the width of the quilt either side of this centre point again with pins. Pin the outer border strips to the top and bottom of the quilt matching the centre points and the outer edge with the marker pins. Stitch, starting and finishing ¼ in/0.75 cm from the edge.

4 Measure the length of the quilt through the centre and repeat with the remaining two outer border strips. Press all seams towards the borders. Mitre the corners as described on page 12.

FINISHING THE QUILT

1 Layer backing, wadding and quilt top. Pin and baste the layers together in a grid, starting from the centre and working outwards.

2 Quilt in the pattern of your choice.

3 When the quilting is complete, stitch the binding strips together as required and use to bind the quilt with a doublefold binding (see page 17).

Liberated Piecing

COLIN BRANDI

I developed this technique, which subsequently became known as 'Liberated Piecing', some years ago while trying to develop a way of making quilts that allowed me freedom to work with the fabric in a spontaneous way, and without the limitations that templates can impose. While I might select the fabrics for colour and pattern before starting on a piece of work, and might have a basic idea of the design, the overall surface of the quilt is allowed to develop as I cut and join the fabric, a process which may be repeated many times before the final selection of an area is made using a window template. In some respects this more resembles painting and drawing than conventional quiltmaking.

The following designs of necessity use a simplification of my usual process but they demonstrate the basic techniques and principles.

Star Crazy

THIS LARGE SOFA THROW OR BED QUILT uses a simple process of cutting and joining the fabric to create a design with a lot of movement. Only three fabrics are used and a careful choice of colour will create different spatial effects. The 'fragmented' border demonstrates some of the potential that 'liberated piecing' has to create exciting areas of pattern and colour.

The quilt plan below and the others that follow are given to show how the blocks are assembled. The overall appearance of your finished quilt will be unlike anyone else's.

Quilt size: 73 x 73 in/185 x 185 cm

MATERIALS
Window template with 14 in/36 cm square aperture
Star and binding fabric: 1¾ yards/1.75 metres, 45 in/115 cm wide
Stripes fabric: 1¼ yards/1.25 metres, 45 in/115cm
Background and border fabric: 6½ yards/ 6.5 metres, 45 in/115 cm wide
Wadding: 75 x 75 in/190 x 190 cm
Backing: 75 x 75 in/190 x 190 cm

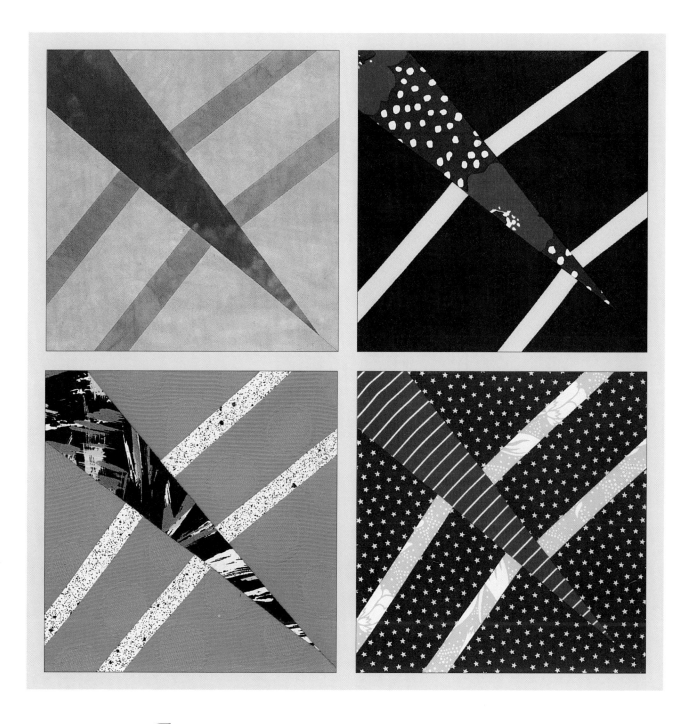

This design was inspired by several nineteenth century star quilts and their makers' bold use of colour. Choosing just three fabrics concentrates the mind on the relationship between them. Don't be afraid of trying unusual combinations or testing the possibility of working with that 'hideous' length of patterned fabric hidden at the back of the cupboard! Combined with two plain or mini patterned fabrics, it might look wonderful.

NOTES WHICH APPLY TO ALL THE PROJECTS

Fabrics: Dress weight 100% cotton throughout, although polycotton sheeting may be used for backings. Wash well before use.

Seams: ¼ in/0.75 cm allowance but the precise amount does not matter, just use the edge of your foot as a guide.

Binding: As an alternative to the separate bindings, which I prefer to use, you can turn an oversize backing to the front. This is a faster method of finishing the quilts.

Wadding: Low loft or needled wadding will be easier to machine quilt. Choose a type which need only be stitched in designs 10 or 12 in/ 25 or 30 cm apart.

Window templates: These are used in all the projects and are all made in a similar way. Start with a piece of stiff card at least 4 in/10 cm larger all round than the 'window', e.g. for a 12½ in/32 cm window the card should be 16½ in/42 cm square or larger. Using a ruler, pencil and set square, draw an accurate 12½ in/32 cm square on the card which will leave a 2 in/5 cm border all round. Using a sharp knife and safety rule, cut out this central window.

CUTTING

1 From the pink star fabric cut a strip, 24 in/61 cm wide across the width of the fabric; place this on the cutting mat and using a ruler, cut 16 long thin triangles, each about 5 in/13 cm wide at the base. Do not measure these; cut by eye

(diagram 1). If you get fewer than 16 from the fabric, simply cut the others needed from the remaining yardage.

1

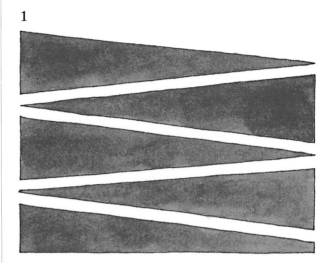

2 From the yellow stripes fabric cut 2 strips, 18 in/46 cm wide across the width of the fabric. Lay these on the board and using the ruler to measure, cut 32 strips, each 2 x 18 in/5 x 46 cm.

3 From the background and border fabric cut 8 strips, 4 x 75 in/10 x 190 cm and 16 squares, 16 x 16 in/41 x 41 cm. **Note:** The long strips should be cut parallel to the selvage.

SEWING

1 Place a background square on the cutting board and, using the ruler, make two straight cuts about 18 in/46 cm long either side of an imaginary diagonal. Do not measure this; work by eye (diagram 2).

2

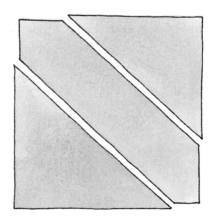

2 Place two yellow strips between the three background pieces (diagram 3). Stitch together the three pieces of the background fabric and the two yellow strips as shown (diagram 4). Press the seams open.

3

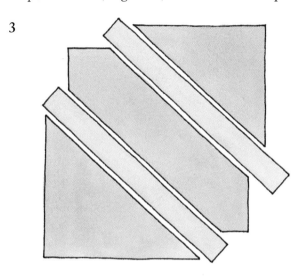

4

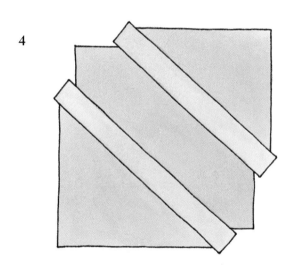

5

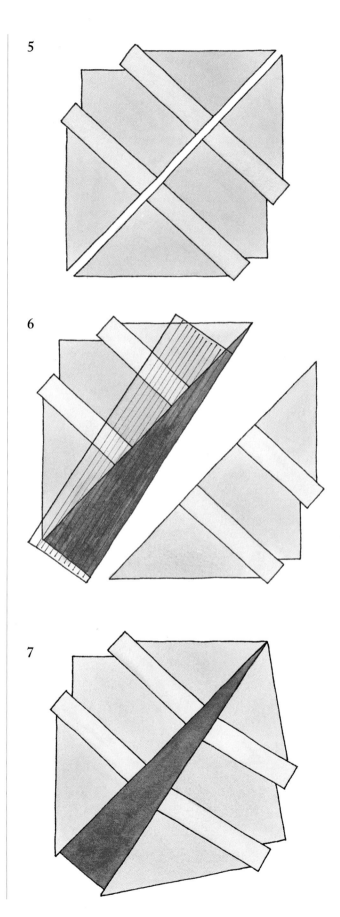

6

7

3 Place the block on the cutting mat and make a straight cut, across the diagonal, at right angles to the yellow stripes (diagram 5).

4 Stitch one edge of a pink triangle to one side of the block. Press the seam open, then straighten the unstitched edge of the triangle using the ruler (diagram 6). Stitch the other half of the block to the triangle and press (diagram 7).

5 Lay the block on the cutting mat and place the window template on top (diagram 8). Mark the corner points with a soft pencil and trim to size, saving all the trimmings for the border (see below). It may be helpful only to use the pencil marks as a guide, using the grid on your board when cutting the block, to ensure that it is cut square.

8

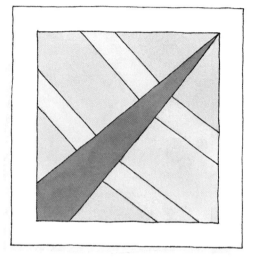

6 Repeat steps 1 to 5 to make the other 15 blocks. The aim is to produce blocks which are variations on a theme, they should not be identical.

7 Arrange the blocks on a 'pin wall' or the floor to form a balanced design (diagram 9) and stitch them together, pressing seams open.

9

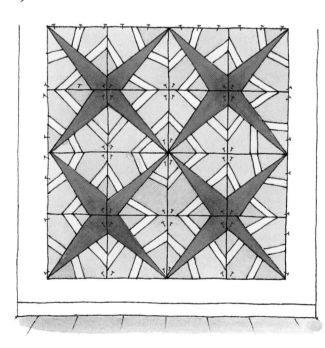

ADDING BORDERS

1 To make the 'fragemented' border, take the trimmings from the blocks and stitch them together (ignoring the grain of the fabric), trimming any ragged edges square and pressing all seams open (and as flat as possible) as you go. The aim is to produce a strip, so add pieces at any angle to achieve roughly this shape.

2 Continue this process until you have a piece of 'new' fabric about 15 in/38 cm long (diagram 10).

10

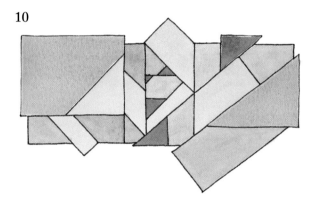

3 Using the ruler, cut one or more rectangles 3 in/8 cm wide and whatever length the pieced fabric will allow (ignoring the grain of the fabric), but note that the ends must be square (diagram 11).

11

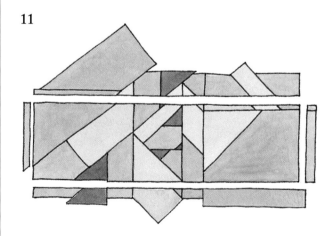

4 Recycle any sizeable trimmings as you make these border pieces and use some of the spare yardage if necessary; this will give you a greater variety of shapes and a more exciting border.

5 Stitch together enough of these short lengths to make the fragmented borders, you will need two lengths 62 in/158 cm long, and two lengths 67 in/170 cm long.

6 Stitch on the three sets of borders to the sides first, then top and bottom, with butted edges (see page 12). Add a plain border first using the background fabric, then the fragmented borders and finally another plain border.

FINISHING THE QUILT

1 Put the top, wadding and backing together (see page 14) and machine quilt 'in-the-ditch' (sinking the quilting stitches in the seams) or use the seam-lines as guides for outline quilting.

2 Trim and bind the edges with a doublefold binding cut from the remaining the pink fabric to finish (see page 17).

Snakes and Ladders

THIS SINGLE BED QUILT USES BOTH conventional strip piecing and a 'liberated piecing' technique to produce the 24 ladder blocks. Any scraps can be sewn together, then cut up to form interesting new blocks for cushions and other small projects. I used mainly Dutch wax prints for the patterned fabrics but any interesting combination of plain colours or prints will work.

Quilt size: 60 x 84 in/152 x 213 cm

MATERIALS
Window template with 12½ in/32 cm square aperture
Patterned fabrics or scraps: 8 fat quarters. (Try to

find an interesting selection of patterns and colours. You may not need all of this fabric but the quantity is important for variety.)
Plain cotton fabric: 5¾ yards/5.2 metres (45 in/115 cm wide) for background fabric
Black cotton fabric: ¾ yards/0.6 metres (45 in/115 cm wide)
Wadding: 62 x 86 in/157 x 218 cm
Backing: 1¾ yards/1.75 metres (96 in/244 cm wide). Sheeting is best for speed since this does not have to be joined
Binding: ¾ yard/0.6 metre (45 in/115 cm wide). I used one of the patterns from the ladders. This amount allows for a doublefold binding 2½ or 3 in/6 or 8 cm wide before folding

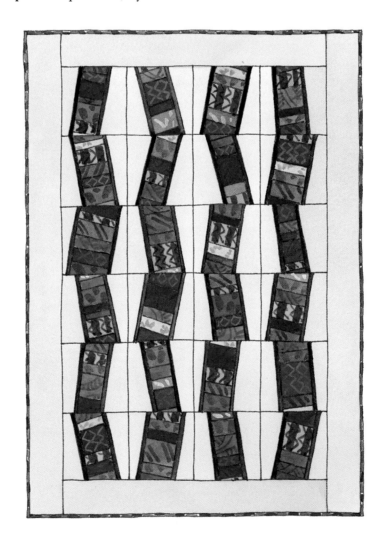

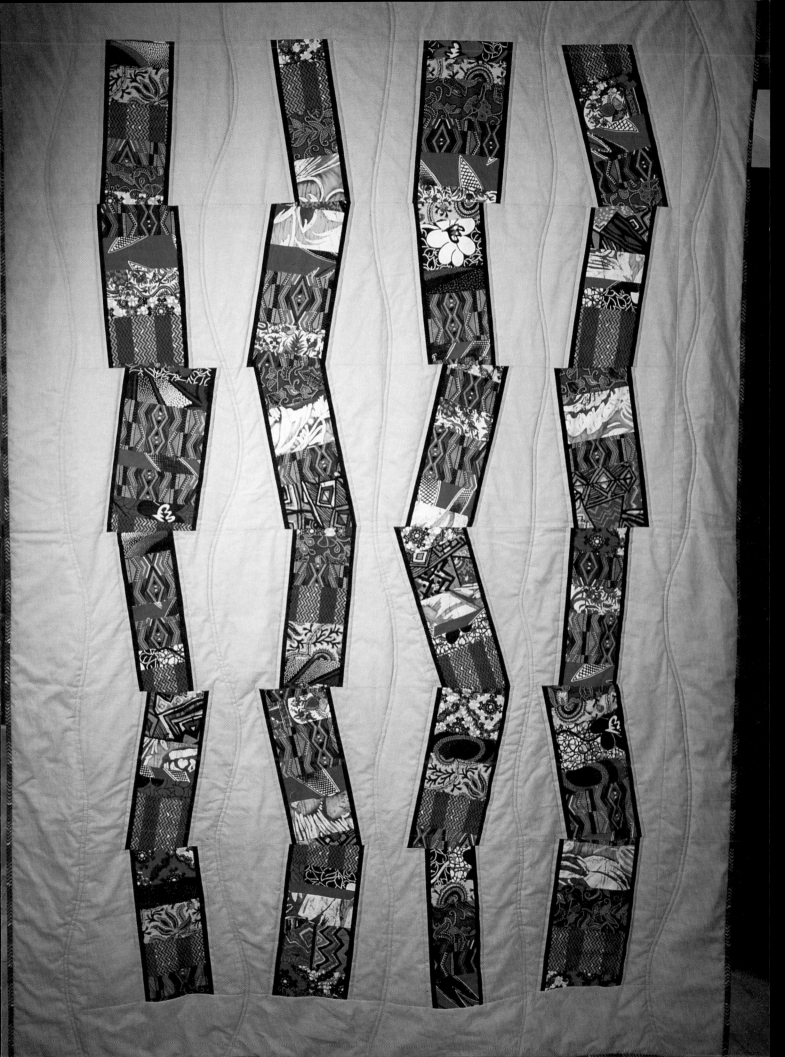

CUTTING

1 Divide the patterned fabric at random, into strips of various sizes from 1½ to 6 in/4 to 15 cm, across the widest part of the panel, i.e. each strip will be about 22 in/56 cm long.

2 From the plain fabric for the background and borders, parallel to the selvage, cut 2 strips, 6½ x 86 in/17 x 233 cm; 2 strips, 6½ x 50 in/ 17 x 127 cm and 16 strips, 6 x 45 in/15 x 114 cm.

3 From the black fabric cut 16 strips, 1¼ x 45 in/3 x 114 cm, across the width for economy but it is always better to cut such strips parallel to the selvage whenever possible.

SEWING

1 Stitch patterned strips of fabric together, at random, to make two panels, each 45 in/114 cm long. Press these panels with seams open; this makes cutting and construction easier. Trim one long edge straight, then divide each panel into four strips of random width between 4 and 7 in/10 and 18 cm (diagram 1).

1

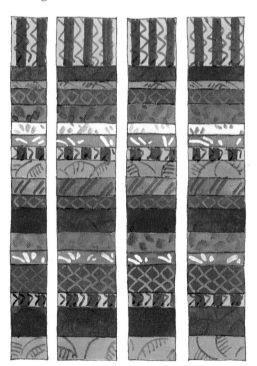

2 Stitch a strip of black fabric to one long edge of each 45 in/115 cm strip of background fabric. Press seams open.

3 Stitch patterned strips to the black edge of the background strips. Press seams to black strip. You will now have eight panels, each of which will give three blocks (diagram 2).

2

Cutting blocks

1 Place a panel on a hard surface, such as a table top, and using the window template mark the corners of the three blocks. Do this with a soft pencil, making two short lines at each corner. At first make very light marks until you are satisfied with the positions (diagram 3).

Important: Vary the position and angle of the window each time you mark a block; the aim is to produce variations on a theme - each block should be an individual design.

3

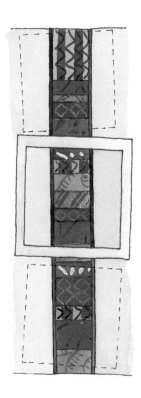

2 Using a long ruler, cutting mat and the rotary cutter, join the points and cut out the three blocks.

3 Repeat steps 1 and 2 with the other seven panels. Note that the ladders in twelve blocks lean to the left and to the right in the other twelve.

COMPLETING THE QUILT TOP

1 Arrange the blocks on a 'pin wall' or the floor, changing the positions until you are satisfied with the arrangement.

Note: You may find it helpful to mark in some way the position of each block once you are satisfied with the arrangement. I use pins with coloured heads, say red for row one and green for row two, and so on. The pins are placed at the top left hand corner, one for the first block, two for the second etc. Providing you record your code on a piece of paper this system prevents blocks being jumbled up, even if you have to put them to one side overnight.

2 Join the blocks together in the usual way: stitch rows of four together, press seams, then join the rows, pressing seams as you go.

3 Attach the border strips, short sides first, with butted edges (see page 12) marking the exact size before you pin them, as measured across the middle of the quilt. This will help prevent a wavy edge.

FINISHING THE QUILT

1 Mark the top for quilting. The quilting lines are in parallel pairs about 1 in/2.5 cm apart, running the length of the quilt, between the ladders and on the borders, in sinuous curves which can easily be drawn freehand. (As an alternative to pencil marking, you can use narrow masking tape as a guide, but this would be put in position after tacking the layers of the quilt together.)

2 Put the top, wadding and backing together (see page 14) and machine quilt using a bright thread and a 'walking foot'.

3 Trim and bind the edges with a doublefold binding, cut $2^{1}/_{2}$ or 3 in/6 or 8 cm wide, before folding to finish (see page 17).

DOUBLE BED QUILT VERSION

This quilt can be made as a double bed quilt 84 x 84 in/213 x 213 cm or larger, if you increase the size of the borders. You will need to make 36 blocks.

MATERIALS
Various colours: 12 fat quarters
Background fabric: 8 yards/8 metres (or more if the quilt is to be greater than 84 x 84 in/ 213 x 213 cm)
Black fabric: 1 yard/1 metre
Wadding: 86 x 86 in/218 x 218 cm (or larger if required)
Backing fabric: 86 x 86 in/218 x 218 cm (or larger if required)

Edinburgh Rock

THIS QUILT ALSO USES BOTH
conventional strip piecing and a 'liberated
piecing' technique to produce the 'strata' blocks
inspired by rock formations on the north-east coast
of the Isle of Skye in Scotland. The size allows it to
be used as a large sofa throw or a bed quilt. Plaid
and striped fabrics were used, and my aim was to
create an interesting surface 'texture' rather than a
conventional pattern of shapes.

Quilt size: 72 x 72 in/183 x 183 cm

MATERIALS

Window template with 12½ in/32 cm square
aperture
Plaid and striped fabrics: a selection of 12 long
quarters for the 'strata' blocks. You may not use all
the fabric but the selection is needed for variety.
Plaid background and border fabric:
2½ yards/2.5 metres, 60 in/152 cm wide
Wadding: 75 x 75 in/191 x 191 cm
Backing: 75 x 75 in/191 x 191 cm
Plaid binding: ¾ yard/0.6 metre contrasting plaid
fabric

CUTTING

1 Divide the plaid and striped fabrics at random, into strips of various sizes from 1½ to 6 in/4 to 15 cm, across the widest part of the panel, i.e. each strip will be about 45 in/115 cm long.

2 From the background and border fabric, parallel to the selvage, cut 2 strips, 6½ x 63 in/17 x 160 cm; 2 strips, 6½ x 77 in/17 x 196 cm and 12 squares, 12½ x 12½ in/32 cm.

SEWING

1 Stitch strips of plaid and striped fabric together, at random, to make two panels, each 30 x 45 in/ 76 x 115 cm. Press these panels with seams open; this makes cutting and construction easier.

2 Cut the panels into strips, of random width from about 3 to 7 in/8 to 18 cm, across the seam lines and slightly askew. Do this by eye; do not measure them (diagram 1).

1

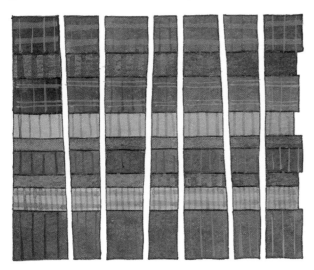

3 Keeping the strips in order, stitch them back together but move each strip down a little - like the fault lines in rock. Vary this displacement from about ½ to 1 in/1.5 to 2.5 cm. You will end up with a zig-zag edge on the two long sides of the panel (diagram 2). Press the seams open.
Note: You will also need to make a smaller panel in the same way about 15 x 18 in/38 x 46 cm; this is for the 13th block.

2

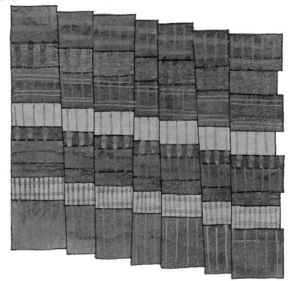

Cutting blocks
1 Place a panel on a hard surface, such as a table top, and using the window template, mark the corners of the six blocks. Do this with a soft pencil, making two short lines at each corner. At first make very light marks until you are completely satisfied with the positions.
Important: Vary the angle of the window each time you mark a block; the aim is to produce variations on a theme - each block should have an individual design.

2 Use a long ruler, cutting mat and the rotary cutter to join the points and cut out the blocks (diagram 3).

3

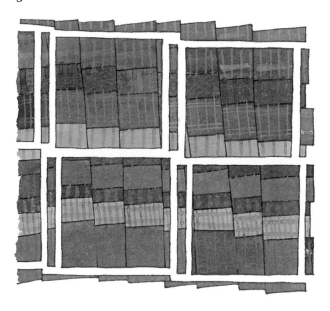

3 Repeat steps 1 and 2 with the other panels; of course the small panel will only yield one block.

COMPLETING THE QUILT TOP

1 Alternate the plaid background squares and pieced blocks on a 'pin wall' or the floor to produce a balanced design, changing the positions of the pieced blocks until you are satisfied with the arrangement.
Note: See the comment in the instructions for the 'Snakes and Ladders' quilt about marking the location of blocks.

2 Join the blocks together: stitch rows of five together, press seams open, then join the rows, pressing seams as you go.

3 Attach the border strips with butted edges in the usual way (see page 12).

FINISHING THE QUILT

1 Put the top, wadding and backing together (see page 14) and machine quilt following the seam lines of the blocks. A straight stitch is used and there are two lines of quilting either side of the seam. I used four different colours to echo the weave in the plaid fabric. You can use either the edge of the machine foot to space the quilting lines, or masking tape if you want a wider spacing.

2 Trim and bind the edges with a doublefold binding cut from the plaid binding fabric to finish (see page 17).

Sword Dance

THIS SOFA THROW OR LAP QUILT USES brightly coloured plaid fabrics against a plain calico background with a strip-pieced edging. The vibrant colours evoked memories of my grandmother, who used to tell me how, as a child, she danced the sword dance over crossed fire irons.

Quilt size: 61 x 61 in/155 x 155 cm

MATERIALS
Window template with 12½ in/32 cm square aperture
Plaid fabric: four contrasting pieces, 45 in x 1 yard/115 cm x 1 metre.

Note: This fabric will all be bias cut; if you select a good 'quilting' fabric this should not present a problem; however, if you are worried about the fabric stretching when it is stitched, it can easily be stabilised by the use of a very lightweight iron-on interfacing. This should be attached to the fabric before cutting out.
Calico background and borders: 4½ yards/ 4.5 metres, 60 in/152 cm wide. This must be washed twice at the hottest setting of your machine. This quantity allows for shrinkage which can be substantial.
Wadding: 63 x 63 in/160 x 160 cm
Backing: 63 x 63 in/160 x 160 cm

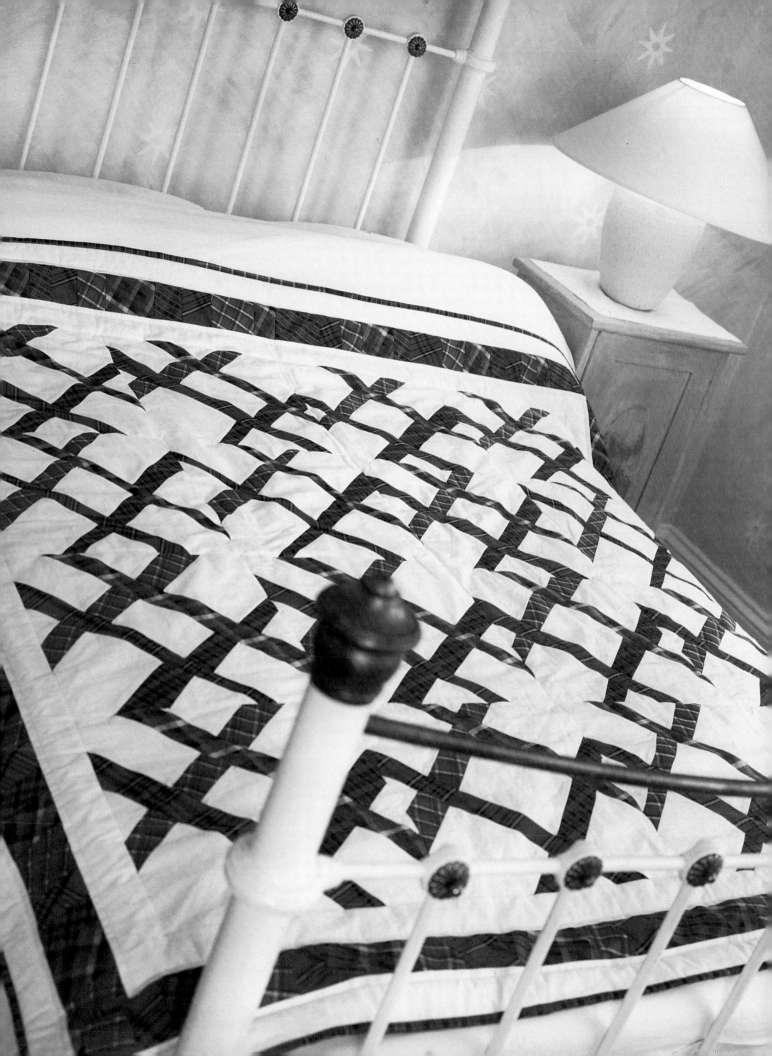

CUTTING

1 From each piece of plaid fabric cut a strip about 16 in/41 cm wide. Lay the four strips, one on top of the other, on the cutting mat and cut bias strips, about 1½ - 3 x 18 in/4 - 8 x 45.5 cm. Do this by eye and do not make any measurements. They should also taper from one end to the other (diagram 1). You will need 16 strips of each colour; if you have not cut enough simply repeat the process.

1

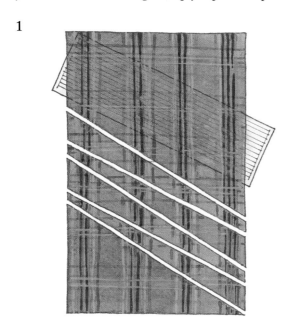

2 Keeping the individual fabrics together, jumble up the strips to ensure a random placing.

3 From the calico cut 16 squares, each about 15 x 15 in/38 x 38 cm; 4 strips, each 2½ x 55 in/ 6 x 149 cm and 4 strips, each 2½ x 65 in/ 6 x 165 cm. **Note:** The long strips should be cut parallel to the selvage.

SEWING

1 Place one of the calico squares on the cutting mat and make four straight cuts to cut out two narrow strips of calico, about ¾ in/2 cm wide (diagram 2). These cuts should be no more than 17 in/43 cm long and although you may need to use the ruler to check this measurement, make the other cuts by eye for a random effect.

2

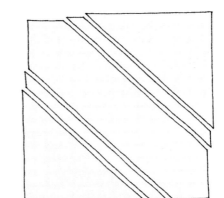

2 Discard the narrow strips of calico. Stitch two contrasting plaid strips in their place. Press seams to the calico; this will enhance the 'inlay' effect and make construction easier (diagram 3).

3

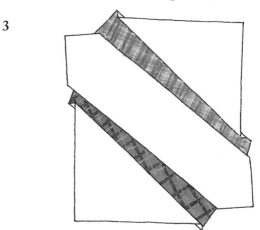

3 Place the block on the cutting mat and make another four cuts approximately at right angles to the first cuts (see step 1 above), again cutting strips about ¾ in/2 cm wide (diagram 4); discard the

4

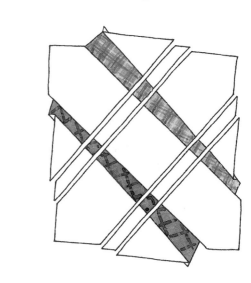

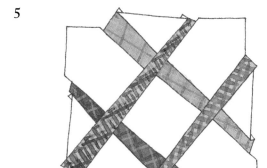

narrow strips of fabric and replace them with strips of the other two plaid fabrics (diagram 5).

5

4 Press the block, with seams pressed towards the calico, then place on the cutting mat. Using the window template as described in the instructions for the 'Snakes and Ladders' quilt, mark and trim the block to size (diagram 6).

6

5 Repeat steps 1 to 4 to make the remaining 15 blocks taking care that you place each plaid fabric in the same position in each block. Remember the aim is to produce blocks which are variations on a theme not identical.

COMPLETING THE QUILT TOP

1 Arrange the blocks on a 'pin wall' or the floor, changing the positions until you are satisfied with the arrangement.
Note: See note in the 'Snakes and Ladders' quilt instructions about marking the location of blocks.

2 Stitch the blocks together in the usual way, pressing seams open as you go.

3 Make the strip-pieced edging by cutting the remaining plaid fabric into bias strips of random width. These are then stitched together, pressed and cut at right angles to the seam lines into 3 in/8 cm widths which can be joined to form pieces long enough for the borders.
Note: You should also have enough fabric to make the binding in a similar way; if not use calico for the binding.

4 Stitch on the first set of calico borders, then the strip-pieced borders and finally the second set of calico borders, pressing seams as you go. (See notes in 'Snakes and Ladders' quilt instructions about avoiding wavy edges.)

FINISHING THE QUILT

1 Put the top, wadding and backing together (see page 14) and machine tie (using the button attachment program or bar tack on your machine if it has one), or tie quilt by hand (see page 16) at the points where the strips of plaid fabric intersect. Machine quilt the borders in a straight line on either side of the pieced border.

2 Trim and bind the edges with a doublefold binding to finish (see page 17) using either pieced plaid fabrics or calico (see step 3 above).

Quick Triangles

PAULINE ADAMS

All seven patchwork quilts in this chapter incorporate triangles, rotary cut and machine sewn in one or more of four different quick ways, one of which is a method of my own devising.

Although all the triangles in these quilts are ordinary right-angle triangles with same-length short sides, the fabric grain lines can run differently. The figures for the metric measurements may look daunting but they are given with the metric rotary ruler in mind. Thus the centimetre is divided into halves, quarters and eighths.

The finishings include machine quilting and tying and there is a variety of edge treatments. Although some of the fabrics I used were remnants or unusual widths, I am assuming that you will be buying from scratch. For the backing, I sometimes used sheeting but this is not recommended for hand quilting, as it is difficult to stitch through. In timing myself, I did not include designing, thinking, deciding-on-fabrics, shopping or fabric-preparation time.

Evening Stars

THE VERY OLD TRADITIONAL FOUR-patch 'Evening Star' block is, when looked at closely, made up of one large square, four little squares and four 'Flying Geese'. The 'Flying Geese' rectangular units are composed of two small 'sky' triangles sewn to one large 'goose' one. Because of the bias seams involved, it is not an easy pattern to sew accurately on the machine. Some years ago I invented a way of making four Flying Geese from five rotary-cut squares which makes them quick, easy and accurate. It's a little bit like a conjuring trick, and almost addictive to do. One 'recipe' of geese makes four geese units to sew into a strip or incorporate in a block.

This baby/lap quilt with its bright sunflower fabric took me 8½ hours to make.

Quilt size: 55 x 55 in/137.5 x 137.5 cm

MATERIALS
All fabrics used in the quilt top are 45 in/115 cm wide

Stars fabric: ¾ yard/70 cm
Inner and alternate border fabric: 1¼ yards/ 1.2 metres
Outer and alternate border fabric: 1½ yards/ 1.4 metres
Wadding: 1¾ yards/1.5 metres 2 oz polyester, 60 in/152 cm wide
Calico backing: 1¾ yards/1.5 metres, 60 in/ 150 wide
Double knitting yarn for ties

These little collages show a series of alternative fabrics for the Evening Star block. A two-colour version gives twinkling star points, whereas the three-colour set with dark fabric gives less emphasis to the points. The three-colour block with maroon squares would work well alternated with plain squares and the solid-coloured arrangement would produce a very graphic quilt.

93

CUTTING

1 From the star fabric, cut 2 crosswise strips, 5½ in/14 cm wide. Cut these into 9 'A' squares.

2 Cut 3 strips, 3⅜ in/8.875 cm wide. Cut these into 36 'sky' squares.

3 From the inner border fabric, cut 2 crosswise strips, 6¼ in/16.25 cm wide. Cut these into 9 'geese' squares.

4 Cut 5 strips, 5½ in/14 cm wide. Cut these into 4 'F' borders, 10½ in/26.5 cm long and 4 'H' borders, 30½ in/76.5 cm long.

5 From the outer border fabric, cut 8 crosswise strips, 5½ in/14 cm wide. Cut these into 4 'I' borders, 35½ in/89 cm long; 4 'G' borders 15½ in/39 cm long; 12 'D' squares, and 20 'E' rectangles 3 in/7.75 cm wide.

SEWING

1 Make nine recipes of 'Flying Geese' with 'geese' and 'sky' squares (see page 114).

2 Following the stitching plan (diagram 1), first stitch 20 'E' rectangles to geese rectangles, then make up the different strips as shown, and assemble the made-up strips in the order given. You will notice that the central square is stitched first and pairs of borders added first at sides, then at top and bottom. Finger-press all seams until the whole is completed, then press.

1

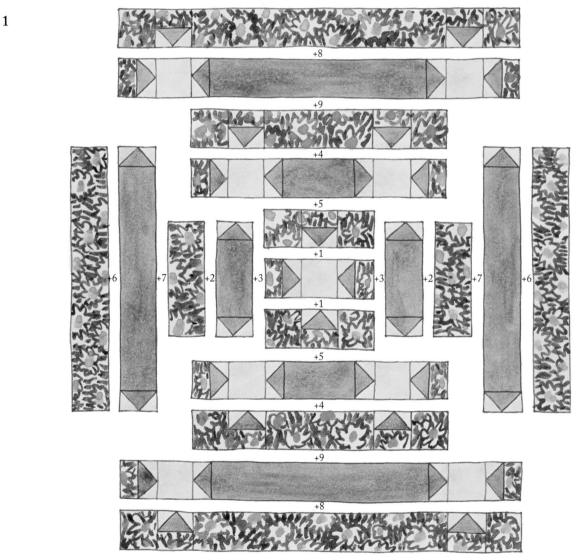

94

FINISHING THE QUILT

1 Layer with wadding and backing for bagging-out (see page 13).

2 Turn, close opening and stitch all round, ¼ in/0.75 cm from edge.

3 Tie (see page 16) with yarn in the centres of 'A' squares, corners of 'D' squares, centre of bottom edge of 'geese' and evenly along centres of borders.

Marching Windmills

THIS SINGLE BED QUILT FEATURES AN old pattern, also known as 'Pinwheel'. Here it forms part of a nine-patch block in a 'Single Irish Chain' layout, marching across the quilt top to the corners. I used six dark print and plain fabrics in browns, blues, purple and orange and six light prints in pale corals, yellows and beige, deliberately choosing fabrics of different scales of pattern and some of more medium tones to get a more ambiguous patchwork effect, with a light beige print for the background and borders.

Fat quarters are a useful size for the triangle piecing method. To get the maximum random effect with so few fabrics, I chose to direct-cut the triangles, i.e. to cut the triangles with the rotary cutter (see below). If you choose to use just two fabrics for the small windmill squares and perhaps a third for the background small and large squares, then half-square Johannah-gridded-triangles (see page 103) would be a good alternative choice of piecing method. With quite small patchwork pieces and machine quilting to match, the quilt took nearly 26 hours, just over half this time was taken in cutting and sewing, the rest in quilting and finishing. You could reduce this time by combining tying and quilting, or even more by only tying.

Quilt size: 64$\frac{1}{4}$ x 89$\frac{3}{4}$ in/163 x 227.5 cm

MATERIALS
All fabrics used in the quilt top are 45 in/115 cm wide
Light fabrics, prints and plain: 6 quarter-yards (20 cm) or 6 fat quarters, or equivalent in scraps to total 1 yard/1 metre
Dark fabrics, prints and plain: 6 quarter-yards (20 cm) or 6 fat quarters, or equivalent in scraps to total 1 yard/1 metre
Background and border fabrics: 4 yards/4 metres
Wadding: 67 x 92 in/168 x 233 cm or 1 quilt sized piece, in 2 oz polyester
Backing: 3 yards/2.7 metres sheeting, 90 in (2.3 m) wide

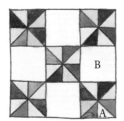

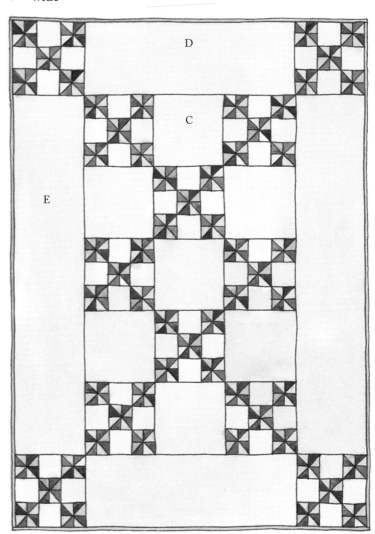

CUTTING

1 From the light and dark fabrics, cut strips 3 in (8 cm) wide.

2 Cut these into 3 in (8 cm) squares (total: 120 dark squares and 120 light squares).

3 Cut these squares across diagonally once to form 'A' triangles (see quilt plan on page 96).

4 From the background fabric, cut 6 crosswise strips, $4^3/4$ in/12.25 cm wide and cut into 48 'B' squares.

5 Cut remaining background fabric into 3 lengthwise strips, $13^1/4$ in/33.75 cm wide.

6 From these strips cut 2 'E' borders $64^1/4$ in/ 162.75 cm long, and 2 'D' borders $38^3/4$ in/ 98.25 cm long.

7 Cut 7 'C' squares from remaining strips. If you decide to make direct-cut triangles (see below), for 'half-square triangles', cut squares $^7/8$ in/2.625 cm bigger than required finished size, and cut across once diagonally. Stitch into pairs on the long side with scant $^1/4$ in/0.75 cm seam. For 'quarter-square triangles', cut squares $1^1/4$ in/ 3.75 cm bigger and cut across both diagonals. Stitch into pairs, then squares, to suit pattern.

Direct cutting

This means rotary cutting all the patchwork pieces to the shapes and sizes needed, without the use of templates or pencilled cutting lines. No marked stitching lines are needed either: line up the fabric edges with the edge of the sewing machine foot or a mark on the machine throat plate - whichever is a scant $^1/4$ in/0.75 cm from the needle.

SEWING

1 Here, the direct-cutting of half-square triangles has already been done. Keep the cut triangles in separate piles of each fabric. You are aiming to get maximum mixing in the piecing, so make a new working pile of six of one light and one each of the six dark fabrics.

2 Stitch one light to one dark triangle from this pile, along their long sides. Chain-piece (see page 12) remaining triangles in the pile and make new piles with each different light fabric in turn until all the 'A' triangles have been used up. Snip apart, open out squares and finger-press (see page 12) seams under dark fabric.

3 To get a good colour arrangement, place these triangle-squares into sets of four in the windmill layout (diagram 1). Stitch upper squares to each other, then lower squares similarly, nestling seams (see page 12), pinning if necessary and finger-pressing seams to the light side this time.

1

4 Pin, then stitch pairs of squares together, matching centre crossing-point of seams to make 60 windmill squares. Tame seam crossings as described below.

5 Make 12 nine-patch blocks by stitching windmill squares alternately with small background 'B' squares. Use five windmill blocks and four 'B' squares (diagram 2). Finger-press seams towards background fabric.

2
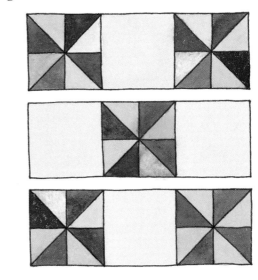

Tame seam crossings

Eight seams meet in the middle of these pinwheels and can form a nasty lump. If they all lie in the same direction the lump goes. To enable the last seam sewn to lie similarly, unpick a few stitches within the seam allowance of the two seams at right angles to it. Do this carefully, being sure not to unpick nearer the seam allowance than one stitch. Trim off any projecting triangle points (diagram 3) and press.

3
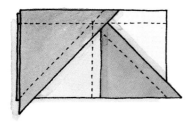

COMPLETING THE QUILT TOP

1 Still always using a scant ¼ in/0.75 cm seam allowance, and pinning where necessary, stitch one large windmill block to each end of the two short border 'D' strips.

2 Stitch remaining windmill blocks alternately with large background 'C' squares to form five sets of three (see quilt plan). This will make the central part of the quilt top.

3 Stitch on side 'E' borders and finally the top and bottom borders. Press.

FINISHING THE QUILT

The quilting is done in two stages to minimize slippage and puckering between the three layers of the quilt.

1 Spread out the wadding and place quilt top smoothly on it, right side up, leaving 2 in (5 cm) minimum of wadding projecting on each side. Safety-pin layers together.

2 Use white thread in the machine bobbin and top thread matching background fabric. Lower,

disable or cover machine feed dogs, and set machine to zero stitch length to do free machine quilting (see page 15). Outline-quilt all windmill dark triangles.

3 Spread out backing wrong side up and place quilted top smoothly over it, with 2 in (5 cm) of backing projecting beyond quilt top edge. Re-pin.

4 Mark a cross in the centre of all 'B' squares, nine in equivalent positions in large 'C' squares, and in the same spacing on the borders. With bobbin thread matching backing, and top thread still matching background, free machine-quilt small windmills at each marked point, by starting in the middle and making first one then another spiky figure-of-eight (diagram 4). Trim off threads.

4

5 Trim wadding flush with quilt top. Trim backing ½ in (1.5 cm) larger all round than quilt top, and make a lapped edge by turning the excess backing to the front and machining down with ¼ in/0.75 cm turning, trimming excess inside corners as necessary.

ALTERNATIVE SIZE

To make a double bed quilt, 94 x 94 in/ 227 x 227 cm square would need 17 pieced blocks and 12 'C' blocks. Buy 8 fat quarters each of light and dark fabrics and cut 170 'A' squares each of lights and darks. Buy an extra 2 yards/2 metres of background fabric. First cut 'B' squares from crosswise strips, then 2 crosswise strips to join for one 'D' border. Cut 3 lengthwise border strips 'D' and finally 12 'C' squares. A king-size wadding would be needed, and backing fabric would have to be pieced to make a square about 95 x 95 in/ 241.5 x 241.5 cm.

Whirligig

A S MIGHT BE EXPECTED FROM THE large pieces, smaller size and tied finish, this is a real quickie of a quilt, which took less than six hours to make; less than half of this was used in piecing. It uses the same 'Pinwheel' pattern as the previous quilt, but on a much, much larger scale. It is coloured to be a lap or knee quilt rather than the similarly sized baby quilts.

The 'Johannah-gridded-triangle' methods used here were developed before the days of the rotary cutter, but remain both accurate and useful, especially when making many triangles of only two fabrics. There are versions for both half-square and quarter-square triangles. The half-square technique is used for the triangles in the narrow border corners, and the quarter-square techniques for the pinwheel triangles, because they are set on point and this way the grain line of the fabric is kept correct. The 'B' triangles are direct-cut.

Quilt size: 60$\frac{1}{2}$ x 60$\frac{1}{2}$ in/151.5 x 151.5 cm

MATERIALS
All fabrics used in the quilt top are 45 in/115 cm wide
Dark fabric: 1$\frac{3}{4}$ yards/1.5 metres
Light fabric: 2$\frac{1}{4}$ yards/2 metres
Backing: 1$\frac{3}{4}$ yards/1.6 metres coloured contrast sheeting, 90 in/230 cm wide
Wadding: 63 x 63 in/157 x 157 cm or 1 double quilt sized piece, in 2 oz polyester
Contrast cotton knitting yarn for ties: double-knitting or 4-ply

CUTTING

Note: Because the pieces are so large, it is easy not to notice a mis-measurement while rotary-cutting, so check with a tape measure that the ruler is positioned correctly and only cut once you are sure.

1 Referring to the quilt plan on page 100 and the cutting layouts (diagrams 1 and 2), from the dark fabric, cut 1 square, $13^{1}/_{4}$ x $13^{1}/_{4}$ in/33.75 x 33.75 cm for making 'A' triangles;

2 squares, $6^{7}/_{8}$ x $6^{7}/_{8}$ in/17.625 x 17.625 cm for making 'D' triangles;

4 strips, $6^{1}/_{2}$ x $24^{1}/_{2}$ in/16.5 x 61.25 cm for narrow borders 'C';

and 4 squares, $12^{1}/_{2}$ x $12^{1}/_{2}$ in/31.5 x 31.5 cm for large corner squares 'F'.

1

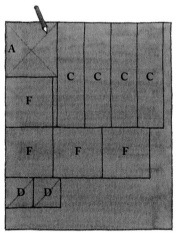

2

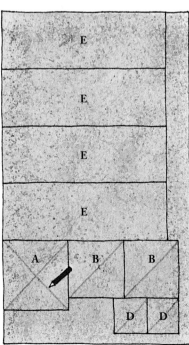

2 From the light fabric, cut one square, $13^{1}/_{4}$ x $13^{1}/_{4}$ in/33.75 x 33.75 cm for making 'A' triangles;

2 squares, $12^{7}/_{8}$ x $12^{7}/_{8}$ in/32.625 x 32.625 cm (cut each of these squares diagonally into two triangles for 'B' triangles);

2 squares, $6^{7}/_{8}$ x $6^{7}/_{8}$ in/17.625 x 17.625 cm for making 'D' triangles;

and 4 strips, $12^{1}/_{2}$ x $36^{1}/_{2}$ in/31.5 x 91.5 cm for wide borders 'E'.

SEWING

1 Make the centre pinwheel of quarter-square triangles using the Johannah-gridded-triangle method (see opposite) by marking both diagonals of the light 'A' square on the wrong side. Pin right sides together with the dark 'A' square and stitch a scant $1/_4$ in/0.75 cm on the anticlockwise side of each diagonal line. Press, then cut on the drawn diagonal lines to yield four pieced pairs of triangles. Finger-press seam towards the dark fabric.

2 Stitch one 'B' triangle to each pair of 'A' triangles. Finger-press seam towards the 'B' triangle. Stitch pieced squares into pairs, finger-pressing seams towards the lighter fabrics. Stitch pairs of squares together, and 'tame' centre seam crossing (see page 99).

3 Stitch two narrow 'C' borders to opposite sides of centre pinwheel square. Press seams outwards.

4 To make half-square triangles, take one dark 'D' square, and mark one diagonal on the wrong side. Pin to a light 'D' square, right sides together, and stitch a scant $1/_4$ in/0.75 cm on each side of the marked line. Cut on the marked line, between the two lines of stitching. Repeat with the other two 'D' squares.

5 Stitch these triangle squares to each end of remaining two 'C' borders, ensuring colour placement is correct, then stitch these borders onto the top and bottom of the centre square.

6 Stitch one wide 'E' border to each side of centre. Stitch corner squares 'F' to each end of the remaining two 'E' borders and stitch onto the top and bottom of the centre. Press.

Johannah-gridded-triangles

1 Decide on finished size of square, and how many are needed. Select two fabrics large enough to accommodate the grid.

2 For half-square triangles, rule on the wrong side of one of the fabrics a grid of squares that are $7/8$ in/2.625 cm larger than the desired finished square size. Draw only half as many squares as the final number needed.

3 Draw in one diagonal on each square. Pin the two fabrics, right sides together, and stitch a scant $1/4$ in/0.75 cm on each side of the diagonal lines only (diagram 3). Press.

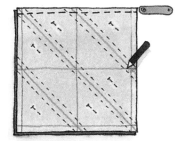

4 Cut (scissors or rotary) first on all the square lines before cutting between the pairs of stitched lines. The few stitches across triangle tips are easily removed before finger-pressing seams.

5 For quarter-square triangles, rule the square grid $1¼$ in/3.75 cm larger than the desired finished square size. Draw the diagonals in both directions.

6 Pin fabrics together and stitch $1/4$ in/0.75 cm from drawn diagonal line. Depending on the required triangle arrangement, stitch on either the clockwise or anticlockwise side of each diagonal (diagram 4), noting that the needle has to be lifted at the end of each line of stitching and moved sideways to the beginning of the next line, or on both sides of one diagonal only. Press. Cut on the square lines first, then on both the diagonal lines.

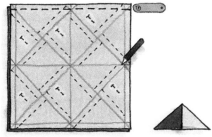

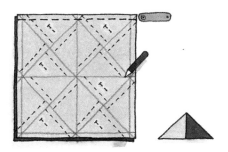

7 It may be more convenient to mark and stitch these triangles, in exactly the same way, but on strips, or on single squares. The rotary mat with its edge measurements, makes a useful place to mark grid squares.

FINISHING THE QUILT

1 Mark positions for ties following the quilt plan (see page 100). Layer the quilt with backing and wadding (see page 14), ensuring that backing and wadding protrude equally on all sides.

2 Tie the quilt. The knot shown is far easier, quicker and more economical of yarn than the more usual knot. It takes far longer to explain than it does to tie. Using a sharp, large-eyed needle and a long length of doubled yarn, tie on marked positions. Take a stitch on the mark, through all layers. Pull yarn through, leaving a 2 in/5 cm tail on top. Flip the yarn in a loop around the back of the tail, then take hold of the tail with one hand while passing the needle up through the front of the loop with the other. Pull tight on needle and tail to close the knot near the quilt surface, then trim off ends to 1 in/2.5 cm (diagram 5).

5

3 Trim the wadding down to the quilt top size and trim the backing to $1½$ in/4 cm larger all round than the quilt top. Finish with a lapped edge (see page 99).

Square Dance Cot Quilt

I DESIGNED THIS BLOCK AND MADE MY first quilt with it in the early 1970s, in lavender and white Laura Ashley prints, for a friend's baby. It was all sewn by hand and I knew instantly that hand-piecing was not for me! The simple block achieves movement by being set on point with alternate plain setting blocks, and has additional interest because the background colour carries over into the block. The fabrics were some I had in the cupboard, a deep pink poplin and a splashy print curtaining which echoes the pink; both were too closely woven for any hand work. The quilt has a narrow border to frame the patchwork, instead of finishing with a time-consuming binding. The quilt took me a total of 13½ hours.

The 'Williamson corner-square' triangle technique used for the centre of these blocks (see page 135) is relatively new to me and I find it increasingly useful. Here it keeps the grain lines running correctly for the block's central square-on-point. It is particularly suitable for corners on squares or on rectangles (flying geese and trape-zoids, for instance) and has no complicated mathe-matics, as the standard ½ in/1.5 cm for seams is added to the pieces used. It leaves smaller triangle cut-offs, which can be used in another project. The technique has been used to attach the 'B' triangles to the 'A' square (see block diagram).

The pink quilting is a new technique I devel-oped specially for this quilt. I wanted to save time by not drawing quilting lines, so I used embroidery yarn as both a guide for the machine quilting and a decoration, couching it down with a long, narrow zig-zag stitch.

Quilt size: 38 x 50 in/95 x 125 cm

MATERIALS

All fabrics used in the quilt top are 45 in/115 cm wide.

Patterned fabric: 1 yard/1 metre
Plain fabric: 2¼ yards/2 metres
Wadding: 1¼ yards/1.1 metres, 2 oz polyester, 60 in/150 cm wide
Backing: 1¼ yards/1.1 metres, calico, 60 in/150 cm wide
Embroidery or crochet yarn: about 33 yards/30 metres, 6-strand

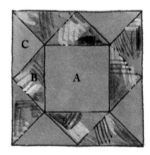

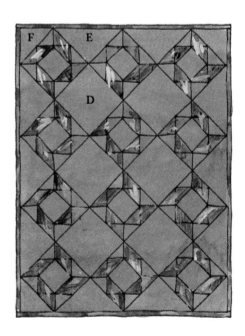

CUTTING

1 From the patterned fabric and following the cutting layout (diagram 1), cut 5 crosswise strips, 1½ in/4 cm wide for borders; from these strips cut 2 strips, 36½ in/91.5 cm long, and from the remaining strips joined to make one long length, 2 strips, 50½ in/126.5 cm long for the borders.

4 (5 for metric) crosswise strips, 3½ in/9 cm wide (cut these strips into 48 squares to make 'B' triangles - this is correct!);

and 3 crosswise strips, 3⅞ in/10.125 cm wide (cut these strips into 24 squares and cut diagonally once into 'C' triangles).

1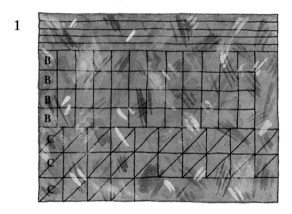

2 From the plain fabric and following the cutting layout (diagram 2), cut 2 crosswise strips, 6½ in/16.5 cm wide (cut these strips into 12 'A' squares - this is also correct);

3 crosswise strips 3⅞ in/10.125 cm wide (cut these strips into 24 squares, and cut diagonally once for 'C' triangles);

1 crosswise strip, 13¼ in/33.75 cm wide (cut this strip into 3 squares, and cut diagonally in both directions to make 10 edge triangles 'E');

1 crosswise strip, 9⅜ in/17.625 cm wide (cut this strip into 2 squares, and cut diagonally once to make 4 corner triangles 'F');

finally from the remaining plain fabric, trim one corner off diagonally, using one 'F' piece as a guide, and cut 6 'D' squares on this diagonal, 9 x 9 in/22.75 x 22.75 cm.

2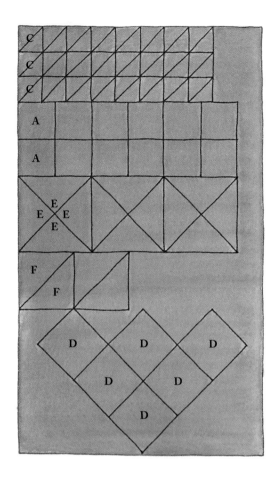

SEWING

1 Mark one diagonal on the back of each 'B' piece. Now using corner-square triangle technique (see page 135), pin one 'B' square in one corner of an 'A' square, right sides together (diagram 3). Stitch on drawn line (from corner to corner of small square) and repeat with remaining 'A' squares, using chain-piecing method (see page 12). Trim corners ¼ in/0.75 cm away from stitching line and finger-press seam towards small triangle.

3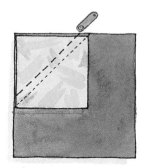

2 Repeat on each of the remaining three corners of 'A' squares. You will be left with 48 small triangles in plain and patterned fabrics to put away for another project.

3 Take one plain and one patterned 'C' triangle. Place plain over patterned, right sides together, and stitch short sides together from square corner to point (diagram 4). Chain-piece the remaining 'C' triangles. Finger-press seams to patterned side.

4

4 Pin and stitch 'C' triangle assemblies to corners of 'A-B' assemblies to complete blocks. Finger-press only, as edges are on the bias and stretchy.

COMPLETING THE QUILT TOP

1 Assemble blocks with alternate plain blocks 'D' and edge and corner triangles 'E' and 'F' (see quilt plan). Work in diagonal rows, finally joining rows together. Press.

2 Pin and stitch the two short border strips to the short edges of the quilt. Pin and stitch the two long border strips to the long sides of the quilt. Press with border seams outwards.

FINISHING THE QUILT

1 Layer the quilt top, wadding and backing (see page 14).

2 Machine quilt (see page 14), with white thread in the bobbin and matching thread on top, around all patterned patchwork shapes, close to seam lines but on the thinner, non-turning side.

3 To couch-quilt the plain areas, it's a good idea to practise the technique before working on the quilt: set the sewing machine for a long narrow zig-zag stitch. Take embroidery yarn and position on

fabric. Pin across yarn to trap it and wrap a 2-3 in/5-8 cm yarn tail around pin as an anchor. Stretch yarn in a straight line to another anchor pin. Both pins should be just beyond desired end of quilted line (diagram 5). Machine-couch with zig-zag stitch the straight line of yarn from beginning point to end. The zig-zag should trap the yarn but not be so wide as to be visible beyond it. Leave needle in down position, remove second pin, raise presser foot and pivot work. Pass yarn around back of needle, then lay it straight in its new direction, pinning just beyond the next turning point. Couch-quilt on next line and continue thus until the star pattern is completed, but leave a yarn tail at completion. Darn yarn ends into wadding layer. Quilt the edge and corner triangles in the same way but with part patterns.

5

4 Finish by trimming wadding the same size as front. Trim the backing about ½ in/1 cm larger than the front. Make a butted edge to finish by turning under a hem of ¼ in/0.75 cm on the front and slightly more on the back, rolling in the edge of the wadding and enclosing it. Stitch close to the edge through both fabrics.

Roman Baskets

THE TRIANGLE TECHNIQUE USED HERE is 'triangles-from-a-tube'. The design for this quilt started out as a bit of lateral thinking. I have often made the 'Roman Stripe' pattern with this technique for very quick quilts. One of the disadvantages of this pattern is that with the usual arrangement of blocks set straight, all the block edges are on the bias and need a straight-grain border to control their stretch. I wondered what would happen if the blocks were set on point. When I drew it the stripped triangles looked just like rows of vases or baskets waiting to be filled. So that is what I did, choosing rather garish colours for the stripping, which repeats in the borders. I used a calico background and naive flowers very simply painted and stamped with fabric paints. An added bonus is that the flowers give an instant quilting pattern. It always amazes me how colours affect each other: when you are choosing fabrics for the stripping (or any patchwork) it is helpful to overlap the fabric bolts to see what they look like next to each other, swap them around until the arrangement is satisfactory. This quilt's size makes it suitable for a throw, a lap quilt or even a wallhanging. I made it in just over 14 hours.

Quilt size: 59½ x 59½ in/144 x 144 cm

MATERIALS
All fabrics for the quilt top are 45 in/115 cm wide.
Five plain fabrics for triangles and border stripping: each ¾ yard/70 cm
Calico background fabric: 2½ yards/2.1 metres
Fabric paints
Wadding: 62 x 62 in/150 x 150 cm or 1 double quilt sized piece, in 2 oz polyester
Backing: 2 yards/1.8 metres sheeting, 90 in/230 cm wide

CUTTING AND SEWING

1 From each of the 5 coloured fabrics, cut 8 crosswise strips, 2 in/5 cm wide. Join these end-to-end and press seams open. Do not cut any calico at this stage.

2 Stitch two different coloured strips together, pinning the start of the second fabric 1½ in/4 cm away from that of the first to stagger the joins. Repeat stepped start with each of remaining colours (diagram 1). Press seams in one direction. Measure width of stripping: if your seam allowances are correctly 'scant', the width will be exactly 8 in/19 cm; if not, it won't be. Mine came out ¾ in/3 mm too small, proving my four seam allowances were each just a little too wide. This is why I recommend not cutting everything out first!

1

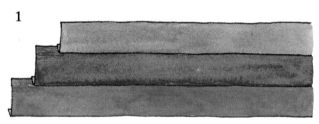

3 Cut 2 crosswise strips of calico to your measured width. Join short ends, press seams open. Place right sides together with stripped piece and stitch both long edges (diagram 2). Press.

2

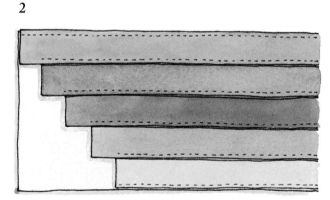

4 Cut 9 triangles from this 'tube' of stripping (see below). It is easiest to use a large triangle ruler; alternatively cut a card template with the height of the triangle exactly matching the width of the stripping, and mark each piece (diagram 3). Unpick the few stitches at triangle points and finger-press seams towards stripping.

3

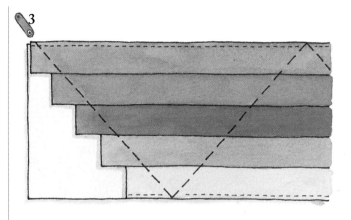

Triangles-from-a-tube

In this quilt the triangles were very large, but they can easily be made any size you want. The resulting pieced squares have bias edges when cut from straight strips (diagram 4a), or straight-grain edges when cut from bias stripping. They can also be made as quarter-square triangles by cutting differently (diagrams 4b, c, and d).

4a

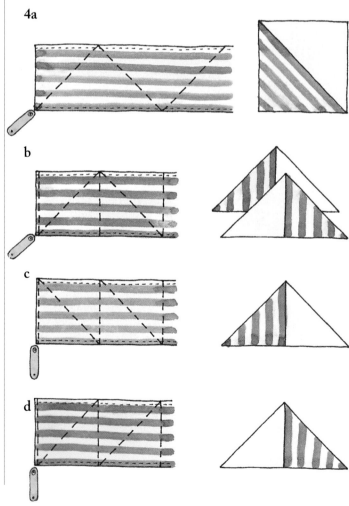

COMPLETING THE QUILT TOP

1 Measure the block sides. Make three thick paper templates for marking the background calico pieces for cutting: one square 'C' to the same size as the measured block side; one triangle 'E' with its long side ³/₄ in/2.25 cm greater than the measured block size, and one triangle 'D' with its short sides ³/₈ in/1.125 cm greater than the measured block size. Label these templates as you make them.

2 Following the cutting layout (diagram 5) cut background calico fabric into 4 alternate blocks 'C'; 8 side triangles 'D' and 4 corner triangles 'E'.

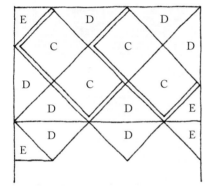

5

3 There are two basket colourways: five of one and four of the other. Lay out all pieces symmetrically. Pin and join in diagonal rows, finger-pressing seams away from stripping.

4 Join the rows following the quilt plan, pinning and nestling seams (see page 12). Tame seam crossings (see page 99). Press. Trim excess from side and corner triangles, rotary-cutting ¼ in/0.75 cm outside the block points. Measure size of patchwork of this centre square top.

5 Add the border. Cut the remaining stripping into four lengths equal to the side length of the patchwork top plus twice the width of the stripping plus 4 in/10 cm (about 64 in/162.5 cm). Mark a dot ¼ in/0.75 cm in from each corner on the back of the calico.

6 Pin first strip to side, with equal amounts projecting at each end. With the quilt top wrong side up, stitch from dot to dot, reversing at seam ends for a few stitches. Pin and stitch the adjacent border stripping on, ensuring the first stripping border is folded clear away when stitching up to marked point. Repeat on remaining two sides.

7 Mitre the borders at each corner. To do this, fold the quilt, right sides together, on a true 45° diagonal through the corner, aligning border seams and edges. Pin. Place a ruler on this fold and mark a continuation of the fold line across the border stripping (diagram 6). Stitch across the stripping, reversing at the end of the seam. Trim excess. Press seam open. Repeat for remaining three corners.

6

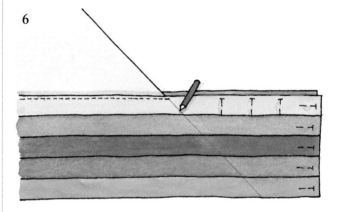

8 Paint, stencil or stamp flowers and leaves in colours of your choice in the triangles above the baskets, using fabric paints.

FINISHING THE QUILT

1 Layer the top and wadding only and secure with safety-pins (see page 14). Quilt against seam lines of border strips (except the inner one) and around baskets. I used invisible nylon thread on top and white cotton in the bobbin. Bag out (see page 13). Re-pin through all layers. Quilt against inner border seam. Using free machine quilting, quilt around all the flowers and leaves. It helps to stretch the flower areas in sections as you work, with a small embroidery hoop.

2 Alternatively, you could stitch additional quilting (about 4-6 hours). Quilt the border strips as before, then mark and quilt vertical lines at the same spacing over the calico squares. Use invisible nylon thread on the coloured areas and white on the calico. Continue as above.

Loop the Loop Geese

FLYING GEESE IS A TRADITIONAL patchwork pattern which is generally made in strips, with alternate patterned fabrics between the strips of geese. 'Flying Geese' also form part of many patchwork block patterns, although they may not always be recognized in a different context (see page 92). They can be used in patchwork in other ways - for instance as arrows or pointers.

In this lap/baby quilt I have taken the traditional strip of geese and arranged it so that it appears to loop over and under itself. The goose fabric - in the large triangles - is a ready-pieced patchwork of Madras checks in vibrant colours and the background of 'sky' to set it off is plain navy. The quilting in the plain areas echoes the looping shapes. It took about 14½ hours to complete.

Quilt size: 57 x 57 in/145 x 145 cm square

MATERIALS
All fabrics for the quilt top are 45 in/115 cm wide.
Goose fabric: 1 yard/1 metre of prepatchworked or patterned fabric (not striped)
Background and border fabric: 3 yards/2.8 metres
Wadding: 1¾ yards/1.6 metres 2 oz polyester 60 in/150 cm wide
Backing: cotton calico 1¾ yards/1.6 metres, 60 in/150 cm wide

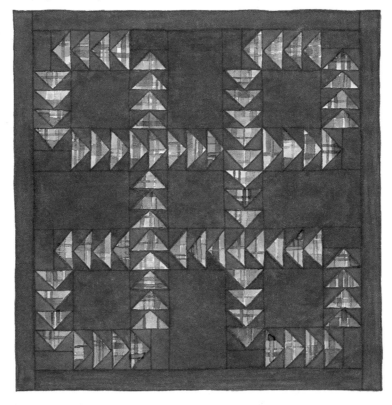

CUTTING

1 From the goose fabric, cut 4 crosswise strips each 7¼ in/18.75 cm wide. Cut these across into 20 squares. Mark both diagonals on right side of each square. These are the 'goose' squares.

2 From the background fabric and following the cutting layout (diagram 1), first cut 4 lengthwise strips, 3½ in/9 cm wide. From these strips cut 2 strips, 51½ in/129 cm long for 'E' borders; 2 strips, 57½ in/144 cm long for 'F' borders, and 12 'B' rectangles, 6½ in/16.5 cm long.

1

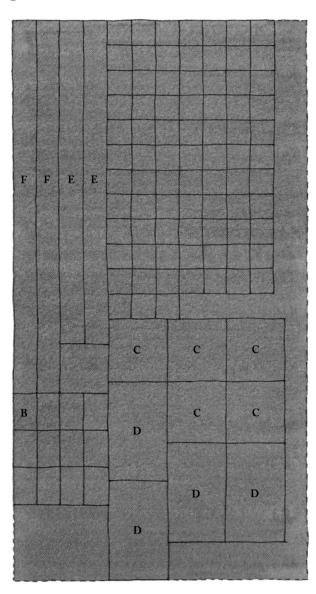

3 From the remaining background fabric, cut 12 crosswise strips, 3⅞ in/10.125 cm wide. Cut these across into 80 'sky' squares, marking one diagonal on the wrong side of each square.

4 Cut 3 lengthwise strips from the remaining background fabric, 9½ in/24 cm wide. Cut these into 5 'C' squares and 4 'D' rectangles, 15½ in/ 39 cm long.

MAKING THE FLYING GEESE

1 Pin a small background 'sky' square to each of two opposite corners of a goose square, right sides together, with the corners exactly aligned, and the diagonal lines on the sky squares in line with the diagonal of the larger goose square.

2 Snip off the corners of the small squares where they cross the middle line and overlap, but no more than enough to stop the overlap (diagram 2).

2

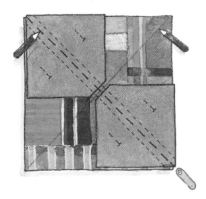

3 Repeat positioning and pinning with remaining goose squares, leaving half the sky squares for the next step.

4 Stitch ¼ in/0.75 cm on each side of the drawn diagonal line on each square, using chain-piecing technique (see page 12), then cut into two sections between the two stitching lines.

5 Take one section and finger-press the two small triangles away from the larger one. Pin a sky square in the corner, diagonal line in line with that under-neath. Repeat with remaining sections. Stitch on both sides of the line (diagram 3), chain-piecing all sections, then cut between stitching lines to reveal two Flying Geese. Finger-press seams away from geese. Do not iron until the geese units have been fully incorporated into the remaining patchwork.

3

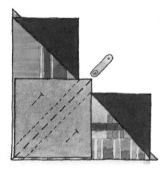

COMPLETING THE QUILT TOP

1 Stitch each of 12 'B' rectangles to the apex of one goose.

2 Stitch geese, pinning first if necessary, into 16 rows of three; two rows of eight and two pairs, all pointing the same way. Finger-press seams towards geese above.

3 Following the stitching order (diagram 4), stitch

4

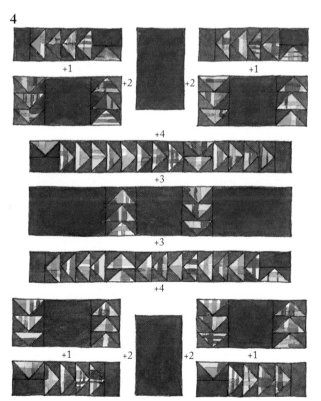

geese strips to background pieces. Stitch sections into horizontal rows, finally stitching the five different rows together. Press.

4 Stitch the two 'E' borders to the top and bottom of the quilt. Stitch the two 'F' borders to the sides. Press.

FINISHING THE QUILT

1 Lay out wadding and safety-pin patchwork top to it. Machine-quilt (see page 14) with top thread matching background and white in the bobbin. This first machine-quilting, without the backing, goes closely around all the geese. It starts in the centre square and, when that is completed, passes out and starts around the outside of a corner loop of geese, inside to the inner edges, then out again - the whole quilting operation can be done in one continuous run.

2 Lay backing on quilt top, pin around edges and bag-out (see page 13). Trace the quilting pattern (diagram 5 overleaf), glue onto card, then cut out.

3 Mark the quilting pattern in the centres of 'C' squares, and in 'D' rectangles. Free machine-quilt (see page 15) each motif. Mark and quilt part motifs in outer sections of 'D' rectangles, having extended them to the border and marked a double line of the same width in the border (diagram 6).

6

5

OPTIONS

1 Different colours. Use five plain colours for the geese (buy fat quarters) in Amish type colours with a black background.

2 Different sizes. The pattern does not lend itself to resizing, except by enlargement or reduction of the size of the patchwork pieces themselves, which would need to be carefully calculated and based on the size of the geese.

   The geese in this quilt measure 3 x 6 in/ 7.5 x 15 cm. Geese are always twice as wide as high. To make other sizes all you need to know is that the squares are cut larger than the desired finished size - the goose square always 1¼in/3.75 cm larger, and the four sky or background squares always ⅞ in/2.625 cm larger. These five squares make one 'recipe' of four geese by the method described. Plain, patterned or checked fabrics are suitable, but not stripes for the geese, unless you want to have two with crosswise and two with lengthwise stripes.

3 Tying. For extra speed, layer and bag-out, then tie the quilt (see page 103). Machine all round the outside of the quilt, ¼in/0.75 cm in from the edge.

Framed Medallion Wallhanging

IN THE EIGHTEENTH AND EARLY nineteenth centuries, before the days of block patchwork as we know it, medallion quilts were all the rage. The centre was either a specially printed picture - a bouquet of flowers, perhaps - or a patchwork. This would be surrounded by borders or 'frames' of printed fabric and/or patchwork. Very often the patchwork fabric was rag-bag stuff, a real mixture of varied precious cotton and linen prints, often being re-used and pieces even being joined to make them large enough. Now nearly all quilt shops and many fabric shops stock printed panels in a great variety of designs. You could even use a printed tea-towel or a motif cut from a furnishing fabric as the centrepiece.

I found this mock patchwork and mock appliqué vase of flowers which appealed to me with its rich glowing colours. It was 16 in/40 cm square which is a fairly standard size. The instructions this time are more explanatory than exact, because panels can be different shapes and sizes.

My first intention was to make this both a sampler of the different methods of making triangles and of different patchwork patterns using only triangles. I soon realised that to achieve this would seriously conflict with the time constraint of making the piece 'in a weekend'. To simplify, I chose the 'Johannah-gridded-triangles' technique. The panel itself was very strongly colour-matched, so I felt it best to use four plain fabrics for both patchwork and borders. Because the centre was too heavily quilted, it pulled together leaving wavy edges. The solution is either to do more quilting in the borders or less in the centre.

Quilt size: 30 x 30 in/76 x 76 cm

MATERIALS
One printed fabric panel: 16 in/40 cm square
Four pieces of cotton remnants: each 12½ in x 2½ yards/31.8 cm x 2.3 metres
Wadding: 1 yard/1 metre, needlepunch (firmer and easier to machine quilt than polyester)
Calico backing: 1 yard/1 metre

1 There are three plain borders and two pieced. For the plain borders I made the inner one wide enough to bring the size up to a multiple of the 2 in/5 cm patchwork squares; the middle border 1 in/2.5 cm to fit the same grid and the outer border a little wider to frame it all!

2 The pieced borders each use two of the cotton fabrics. I used the Johannah-gridded-triangles method (see page 103) in both the half- and quarter-square versions. The inner 'bow-tie' or 'hour-glass' border was made from quarter-square triangles, in a 3¼ in/8.75 cm grid of 18 squares, sewn on the clockwise side of all the diagonals, and the outer 'sawtooth' border from half-square triangles in a 2⅞ in/7.625 cm grid of 22 squares.

Note: Watch that you are joining the triangle-squares together the right way round, especially when adding one border to the next - pin and check before stitching.

3 Because of possible variations in the accuracy of piecing or pressing, you will need to pin and may need to ease edges when stitching the patchwork strips to borders. Remember to add seam allowances on both the patchwork and the borders to allow for the assembly of the quilt.

FINISHING THE QUILT

1 Baste the top, wadding and calico backing together (see page 14). Straight-stitch machine-quilting emphasizes the diagonal lines and borders, and the free machine-quilting outlines the basket and flowers. You can do this with a small hoop used to hold the motif firmly while working.

2 Trim the wadding to size. Lap the front over the back and machine down (see page 99). Attach a fabric sleeve (see page 17) to the back by hand, close to the top edge, and wide enough to take a wooden hanging rod (or stitch curtain rings to the back instead).

OPTIONS

Different patterns. Choose from some of the many patchwork patterns that make suitable borders for a medallion quilt, including squares and rectangles in various formats. A variety, including triangle arrangements are shown (diagrams 1 a to o). Diagrams a to e are pieced from strips; f, g and n are pieced using the Williamson corner-square method (see page 135); h, i and m with half-square triangles using the Johannah-gridded-triangles method (see page 103) and k and l with quarter-square triangles, also using the gridded method. Diagrams j and o use my own 'Flying Geese' method (see page 114).

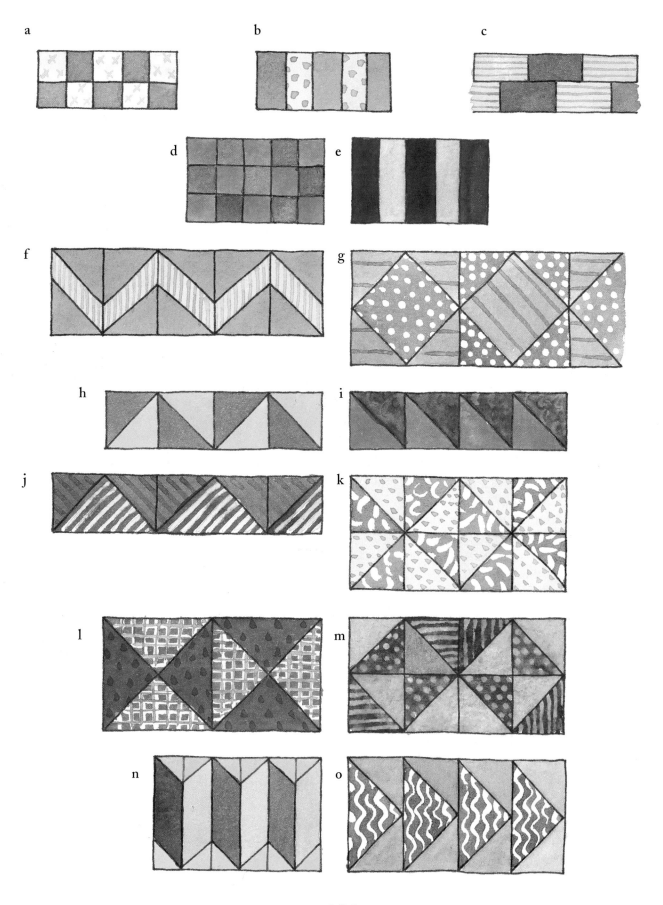

a

b

c

d

e

f

g

h

i

j

k

l

m

n

o

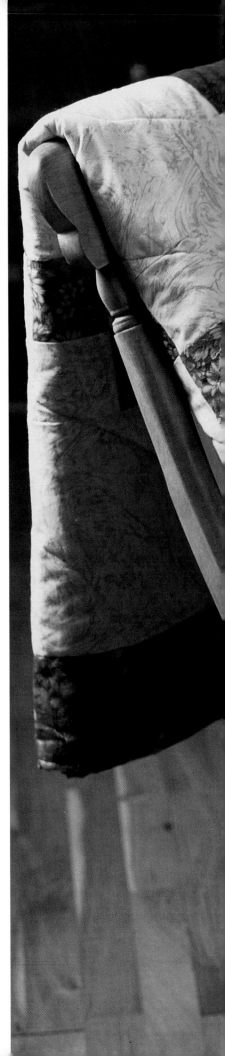

Quick Squares

JENNI DOBSON

*As the projects in this chapter show,
the humble square and rectangle offer the
quilter-in-a-hurry the twin time-savers of
speedy, template-free cutting out and quick
piecing methods, where often some of the cutting is
done after stitching. Yet as they also show, plenty of
possibilities exist in terms of scale and colour
placement for devising attractive and interesting
designs that will display beautiful fabrics to their
best advantage. Making any one of the these
projects is likely to inspire you with ideas for
your own variations and the simple designs are
also ideal for anyone who wants to practise
their quilting on a quickly constructed top.*

Autumn Lanes

THIS IS A VERSION OF THE OLD FAVOURITE nine-patch block called 'Country Roads', which has a single diagonal of three squares highlighted in a contrast fabric. They must have been American country roads to travel in such straight lines! Our single bed quilt shows off some beautiful fruit and leaf prints in autumnal colours to great effect and demonstrates how much well-chosen fabrics can add to a basically simple block. Alternating the pieced blocks with plain setting squares is a good way to increase the size of a quilt quickly but when there is no time to fill these spaces with an interesting quilting design, then the use of a background fabric with a low-key or so-called 'self-pattern' makes good sense.

Quilt size: 82 x 64 in/208 x 162 cm

MATERIAL
Background fabric: 3¼ yards/3.2 metres
Autumn print fabrics: 2¼ yards/2.2 metres of one print for the border as well as some of the blocks, plus 4 fat quarters of other autumn prints
Backing: 4 yards/4 metres
Wadding: 86 x 68 in/218 x 173 cm

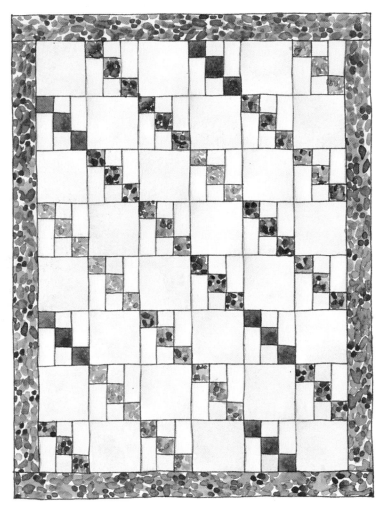

124

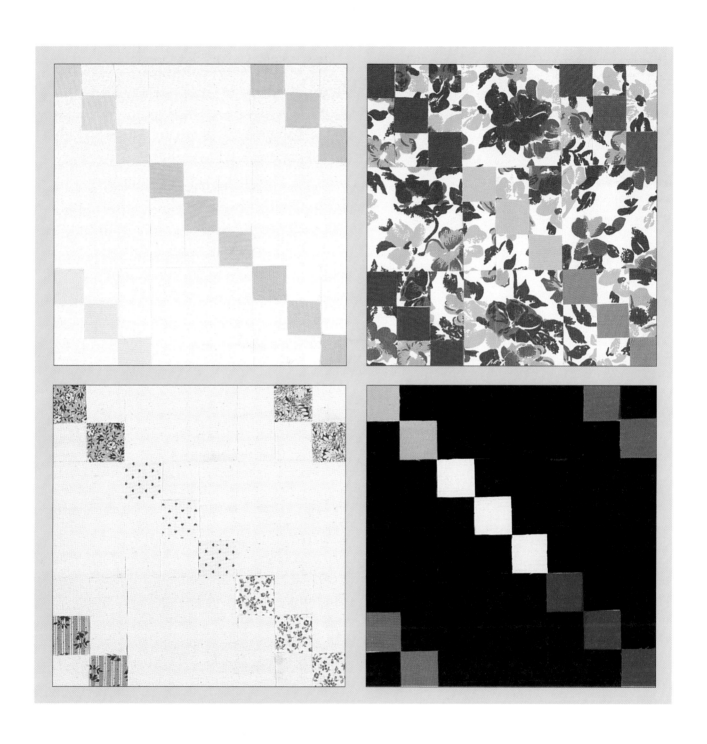

*These collages of different colourways show how changing the colour and pattern of
a fabric can alter the character of any design. Solid colour fabrics produce a graphic
appearance when combined with black or a more delicate look with pastel shades.
Other options are to select a multi-coloured print, then pick out several shades for the
co-ordinating fabrics or to combine a set of period-style designs.*

125

CUTTING

All measurements quoted include a standard $1/4$ in/0.75 cm seam allowance except where stated otherwise.

1 From the background fabric, cut 24 setting squares each $9^{1}/_{2}$ in/24 cm. For the pieced blocks, cut 5 strips, each $6^{1}/_{2}$ x 36 in/16.5 x 92 cm, and 10 strips, each $3^{1}/_{2}$ x 18 in/9 x 46 cm.

2 From the main autumn print for the borders, cut 2 strips, each $5^{3}/_{4}$ x $72^{1}/_{2}$ in/15 x 184 cm and 2 strips, each $5^{3}/_{4}$ x 65 in/15 x 165 cm.

3 From each of the 5 autumn prints for the pieced blocks, cut 3 strips, each $3^{1}/_{2}$ x 18 in/9 x 46 cm.

Note: The instructions below are to make a set of five blocks from each autumn fabric, i.e. five sets of five blocks. As 24 blocks are required for the quilt top, this allows you to play with the appearance of the quilt and so decide which block will be left. This can be used as a label on the back or finished as a cushion to match the quilt.

MAKING THE NINE-PATCH BLOCKS

1 Begin with two of the narrow strips of background fabric. Place one of these, right sides together, with a narrow strip of one of the autumn prints and stitch down one long edge. Press the seam towards the autumn print. Next stitch the remaining narrow strip of background fabric to the other side of the autumn print strip, making sure that the strips are level at one end (see diagram 1). Again press seam towards the print.

1

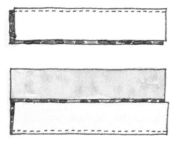

2 Measuring along this pieced strip at right angles to the seams, cut off 'slices', each $3^{1}/_{2}$ in /9 cm wide. It should be possible to cut off five slices with a little bit to spare. Measure and cut carefully to make sure the slices don't acquire a twist. These make the middle part of the blocks (diagram 2).

2

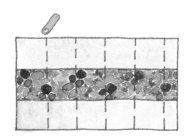

3 Next place the two remaining strips of the same autumn print, one after the other, right sides together along one edge of the wider background strip and stitch. Press seam towards the print. Measure and cut this into five slices each $3^{1}/_{2}$ in/ 9 cm wide as in the previous step (diagram 3). There are now a total of ten slices from both sections of this autumn print (five from each section).

3

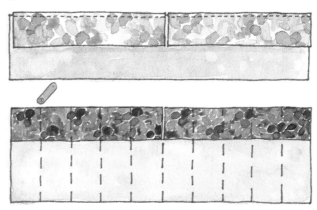

4 To assemble the blocks, stitch together a unit from step 2 and a unit from step 3, matching the corners of the autumn print patches carefully. Make five such pairs (diagram 4). Press. In the same way, add the remaining step 3 units to the other side of the block making sure that the autumn print is correctly turned to complete the diagonal pattern (diagram 5). This completes a set of five blocks all the same. Repeat with the other four autumn prints.

4

5
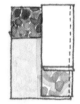 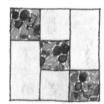

COMPLETING THE QUILT TOP

1 When all the blocks are ready, lay out the background fabric setting squares in a grid using the quilt plan as a guide. Fill the spaces with the pieced blocks, switching them about until you are satisfied with the arrangement.

2 Stitch the blocks together in horizontal rows, then press the seams in opposite directions on alternate rows.

3 Stitch the rows together, matching the block seams on adjoining rows carefully and easing between as required.

ADDING THE BORDERS

1 Press under ½ in/1.5 cm on one long edge of all the border strips. Stitch the two long borders by their remaining edges to the two vertical sides of the quilt. Unfold the pressed-under edge when you add the shorter borders in similar fashion to the top and bottom of the quilt.

2 Press the ends of these strips under to continue on from the pressed sides, trimming to ½ in/1.5 cm if necessary. The outer edges of the quilt should now have a pressed-under ½ in/1.5 cm all round.

FINISHING THE QUILT

1 Divide the backing fabric in half. Place right sides together with selvages level and stitch ½ in/1.5 cm away from one edge. Cut off the selvages and press the seam open.

2 Put the backing, wadding and quilt top together on a flat surface and baste (see page 14). You may wish to use safety pins instead of tacking. They are ideal if you machine-quilt as they are quickly removed as you work. Make sure to use tiny non-staining pins which will leave neither marks nor holes. Be warned that a whole quilt takes a lot of safety pins!

3 It seems a nice idea to contrast the straight diagonal 'roads' of the piecing with winding quilting reminiscent of English country roads! These freely wandering lines are machined along the spaces between the patches, starting and ending at the border. Lastly quilt 'in-the-ditch' round the border (see page 14).

4 Carefully trim the wadding level with the pressed edge of the quilt. Trim the backing to include ½ in/1.5 cm turning. Fold this over the edge of the wadding to enclose it, mitring the corners neatly. Pin in place level with the edge of the quilt top. If you prefer, tack before machining through all layers, close to the edge, to finish. Finally, label the quilt.

Let the Colours Sing

THIS DESIGN WAS ORIGINALLY INSPIRED BY a range of manufacturer's samples; the large simple rectangles of this quilt offer a perfect showcase for a collection of those fat quarters that are so tempting to buy! Their size means that the quilt grows quickly and as little of the fabric as possible is hidden in seam allowances. Novelty and picture prints could also be used effectively in this project. The instructions here are for tying the quilt to finish it, but the design of this single bed quilt is so speedy that it is ideal for anyone who loves to quilt but is less enthusiastic about piecing.

Quilt size: 74 x 72½ in/188 x 182 cm

MATERIALS

Main blocks: 10 fat quarters (offcuts will go towards the border)

Border: 2 fat quarters or equivalent (e.g. 4 fat eighths) to make up the amount needed

Setting fabric: 2 yards/2 metres of navy or any other dark solid colour

Backing: 4½ yards/4.2 metres, or a bed sheet of similar size to the wadding

Contrast colour quilting or embroidery thread for tying

Wadding: 78 x 76 in/198 x 193 cm

CUTTING

1 Remove the selvage from all the fat quarters.
Iron the ten 'showcase' fabrics together in pairs to
speed up the cutting. From the width of the fabrics,
cut a piece 13 in/33 cm wide and divide this into
two 9 in/23 cm pieces along its length (diagram 1).
If you find one fabric is a bit short, either replace it
with one of your border pieces or adjust the size of
all blocks down by the same amount. Save the off-
cuts for the border.

1

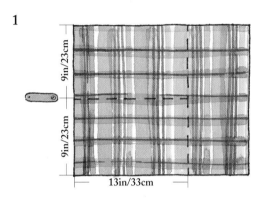

2 From the dark setting fabric cut 2 strips,
4 x 67 in/10 x 170 cm; 2 strips, 4 x 61in/
10 x 155 cm and 4 strips, $3^{1}/_{2}$ x 61 in/9 x 155 cm
(these include a little extra for 'insurance'). Cut 15
strips, $3^{1}/_{2}$ x 9 in/9 x 23 cm. From the remainder
you can cut 2 in/5 cm wide on-grain strips as
required for binding.

SEWING

1 Lay the 20 'showcase' rectangles (two each of
ten fabrics) out in a grid of five rows of four rectangles and organise them into a pleasing arrangement.
Place short setting strips between the rectangles in
each row. Stitch a block to a neighbouring strip and
so on to complete the rows.

2 Lay the four $3^{1}/_{2}$in/9 cm wide setting strips
between the five rows and join these together,
taking special care to line up the showcase rectangles with those on the preceding row.

3 Add a 4 in/10 cm wide strip to the top and
bottom of the assembled centre. Attach the vertical
setting strips across the ends of all the rows.

ADDING THE BORDERS

1 Collect together all the off-cuts from the 10 fat
quarters and sort out the narrowest strip. Divide
this by two to determine the most practical
measurement for the width of your outer border
(diagram 2). In the example illustrated, the border
was cut $4^{1}/_{2}$ in/11.5 cm wide. With a $^{1}/_{4}$ in/
0.75 cm seam allowance and a $^{1}/_{2}$ in/1.5 cm wide
binding, this appears as a $3^{3}/_{4}$ in/9.5 cm finished
border.

2

2 Use the measured width to cut the off-cuts into
pieces of uniform width but of different lengths
(diagram 3). Cut more border strips of the same
width from the other two fat quarters chosen for
the borders. Make sure that you mix the pieces up
well so that you do not inadvertently stitch two
identical fabrics to each other. Don't discard all the
scraps from this process yet. Some may be useful
when you piece together the binding.

3

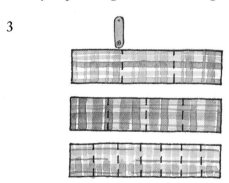

3 Join together the pieces to make four 'Hit 'n'
Miss' borders: two borders 67 in/170 cm long and
two 74 in/188 cm long (diagram 4).

4

2 Tie the quilt layers together at the four corners of each showcase block and once more between, halfway along the long sides using the knot shown (diagram 5).

5

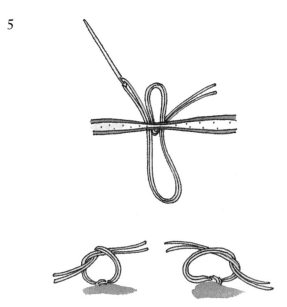

3 Trim the wadding and the backing level with the edges of the quilt top and if there is time, insert tacking to hold the layers together all round the outside.

4 Assemble together strips 2 in/5 cm wide of setting fabric to make up sufficient length for the binding. In our example, since this piecing was a necessity, it was also seen as an opportunity to make the binding more interesting by including a few pieces of the showcase fabrics.

5 Attach the binding with a ½ in/1.5 cm seam (see page 17 but without doubling the binding), then fold it over to the back and stitch into place. Finally, if there is time, add a row of quilting stitches 'in-the-ditch' to secure the inner edge of the border. Don't forget to sign and date your work.

4 Attach the two shorter borders across the top and bottom of the quilt, then stitch the two long borders to the sides (see page 12).

FINISHING THE QUILT

1 Unless the backing is a bed sheet, divide the backing fabric in half. Place right sides together with selvages level and stitch ½ in/1.5 cm away from one selvage. Cut off the selvages and press the seam open. Put the backing, wadding and quilt top together (see page 14).

Rainbow Streamers

IT MAY BE DIFFICULT TO BELIEVE AT FIRST that this cot quilt is cut out completely as squares and no time-consuming templates are required. The triangles appear as if by magic following a method devised by Darra Duffy Williamson. The pieced squares used for the border are a by-product of this method. The basic block of a square with opposite corners cut off diagonally is the one used for a traditional pattern known as 'Indian Hatchet'. However, when it is set with alternate rows staggered by half-blocks, this new twisting diagonal design emerges.

Quilt size: 35 x 47 in/89 x 119 cm

MATERIALS
Background fabric: 1¼ yards/1.25 metres
Rainbow fabrics: 7 pairs of fabric in the colours of the rainbow are required: one light, one dark shade of each colour. Since in some cases only two squares of a colour are required, it might be sensible to use suitably coloured scraps. Otherwise, a fat eighth will be large enough for any of the colours.
Backing: 1½ yards/1.4 metres
Wadding: 39 x 52 in/99 x 130 cm

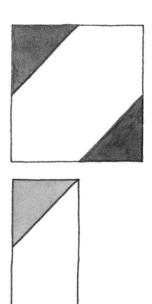

CUTTING

1 From the background fabric and working across the width, cut 6 strips, 6½ in/16.5 cm wide. Cut these across into 6½ in/16.5 cm squares to give a total of 32.

2 Cut 6 half-blocks, each 6½ x 3½ in/ 16.5 x 9 cm from the same fabric.

3 From the rainbow fabrics, cut the following 3½ in/9 cm squares :

Blue: 4 light
              2 dark

Turquoise: 2 light
              4 dark

Green: 5 light
              4 dark

Yellow: 6 light
              7 dark

Orange: 7 light
              7 dark

Pink: 7 light
              6 dark

Mauve: 4 light
              5 dark

4 Cut several strips 1½ in/4 cm wide and as long as possible in different rainbow colours for the binding.

SEWING

1 Place each rainbow square right side down on a firm surface. Fold in half diagonally and finger - press a crease along this diagonal. Be careful not to stretch it in the process! Alternatively a diagonal line may be ruled in with a pencil.

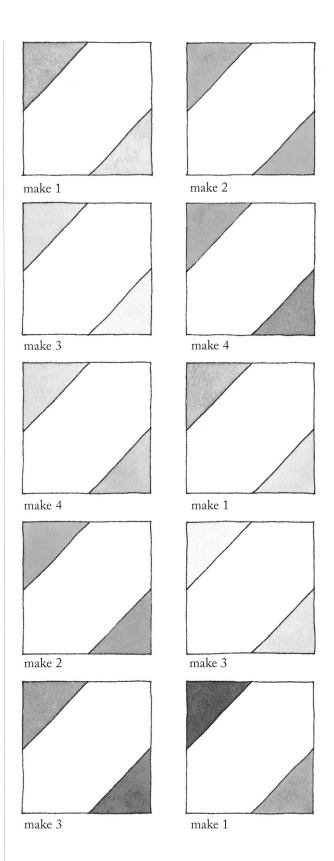

make 1   make 2

make 3   make 4

make 4   make 1

make 2   make 3

make 3   make 1

2   The diagram shows that the blocks have two different colours on opposite corners. Use this diagram to make the blocks in the given colour combinations (diagram 1).

1

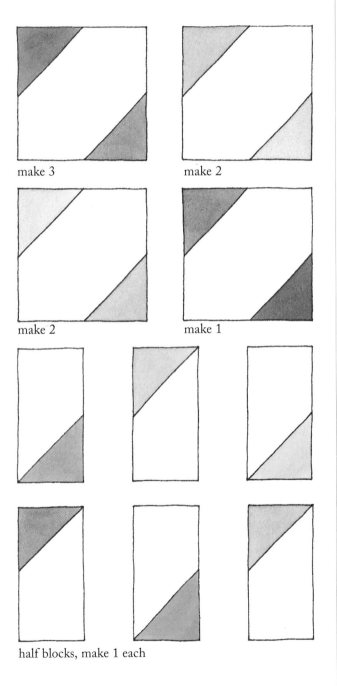

make 3   make 2

make 2   make 1

half blocks, make 1 each

Williamson corner-square triangles

3   To stitch the corner triangles, place a rainbow square, right sides together, on the corner of a background block as shown and stitch accurately on the diagonal fold (diagram 2). It makes sense to work this first step on a set of blocks at a time. This method is 'self-checking': by folding the corner of the rainbow square up towards the corner of the block it's possible to see how well positioned it is. Check the work before proceeding to the next step (diagram 3).

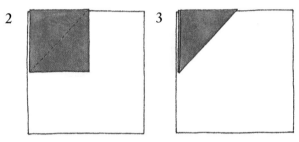

4   Return to the first block and stitch again ½ in/1.5 cm from the first line of stitching, within the corner triangle area (diagram 4). Treat each block in the same way. Press the rainbow corner patches into place and carefully cut between the two lines of stitching (diagram 5). Save the stitched pairs of triangles which have just been cut off.

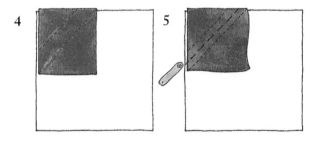

5   Now repeat this step on the opposite corner of the background squares, taking care to add the correct colour to the existing units (diagram 6).

6   In the same way, attach corner triangles to the half-blocks (diagram 7).

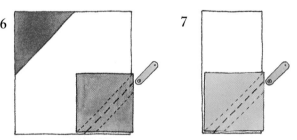

PUTTING THE BLOCKS TOGETHER

1 On a flat surface spread out the blocks in the correct sequence using the quilt plan (see page 132) as a guide. Remember to place the half-blocks at both ends of alternate rows and take care to have them the right way up so that the pattern runs properly.

2 Stitch the blocks together in horizontal rows, pressing the seams in opposite directions on alternate rows, then join the rows together, accurately matching the coloured patches.

ADDING THE BORDERS

1 Return to the stitched triangles and press them all open. These are the squares from which the border is worked. On our example the borders were assembled randomly but a more regular pattern could be followed. However, note that there are not equal numbers of all colours. Other ways of arranging the squares are also possible. Make two sets of 10 squares each for the top and bottom and two sets of 15 squares for the sides. This will not use all the squares but leaves some to play with when working the sets.

2 Lay the pieced border strips out in their correct positions around the quilt and decide which two fabrics will be used in which corners for the frames, then cut two strips, each 5 x 2¾ in/16 x 7 cm and two 7 x 2¾ in/21 x 7 cm from each of the two fabrics for the corners.

3 Stitch a short strip of the appropriate colour to each end of the long borders. Next attach these borders to the long vertical sides of the quilt. Similarly stitch the remaining longer framing strips, one to each end of the short pieced border strips, and stitch them to the quilt. Press the whole top carefully.

FINISHING THE QUILT

1 The flowing design of the twisted streamers is enhanced by a similar quilting design. If you are a skilled machinist the pattern of gentle curves flowing through key junctions of the piecing can be worked without marking. Otherwise make the template shape (diagram 8) shown and use this, with the quilt laid over a firm surface, to mark the quilting lines (see page 13). Alternatively, simply quilt the streamers 'in-the-ditch' (see page 14) which will require no marking.

8

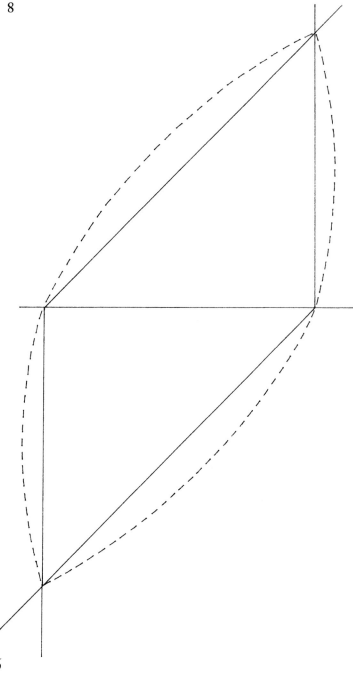

2 Put the backing, wadding and quilt top to together (see page 14). The tacking may be done with safety pins.

3 Work the 'streamers' quilting, then quilt 'in-the-ditch' where the border is attached to the centre.

4 Trim the wadding and the backing level with the quilt top. Bind to finish: a candy-striped binding suits this design well. Stitch the binding strips together, staggering each strip down from its neighbour by the width of the strip (diagram 9). This will form a diagonal end to the set of strips as required for making bias binding.

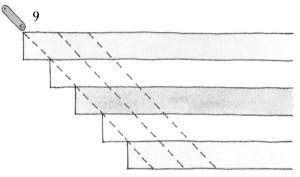

9

5 Sew the binding to the quilt; mitre the corners (see page 17 but without doubling the binding). Finally label your quilt.

SINGLE BED QUILT SIZE

THIS LARGER VERSION HAS 10 BLOCKS ON the top row and a total of 12 rows. Alternate rows begin and end with half-blocks. Begin the colouring sequence with the same light blue triangle. Repeat the same colouring sequence across the quilt - you get nearly two whole repeats.

Quilt size: 64½ x 76½ in/184 x 195 cm.

MATERIALS
Background fabric: 3½ yards/3.2 metres
Rainbow fabrics (light and dark tones of seven colours): 1 long ¼ yard/0.25 metre of each of the 14 fabrics
Wadding: 80 x 68 in/203 x 194 cm
Backing 3¾ yards/3.7 metres

CUTTING

1 From the background fabric, cut 114 squares each 6½ in/16.5 cm and 12 half-blocks, each 6½ x 3½ in/16.5 x 9 cm.

2 From rainbow fabrics, cut 3½ in/9 cm squares according to the following table:

Colour	Blue	Turquoise	Green
Dark	16	16	16
Light	16	16	17

Colour	Yellow	Orange	Pink	Mauve
Dark	19	17	19	17
Light	17	19	17	18

SEWING

1 Proceed as for the cot quilt but make the extra blocks coloured as required.

2 There will be sufficient little pieced squares to construct a similar border design.

3 The backing is divided in half and joined across the middle of the quilt.

Country Garden Four-patch

ONE OF THE SIMPLEST BLOCKS TO SEW, THE four-patch still offers many opportunities for pattern-making. This interpretation uses three sizes of the design within the basic 8 in/20 cm block to build diagonal lines of variously sized squares. By setting with squares of the background fabric, the quilt grows speedily.

Its white-on-white background combined with the smudgy, watercolour floral prints give the quilt a charmingly fresh, outdoor feel. It works well as either a throw or a topper quilt for a single bed.

Quilt size: 48 x 64 in/122 x 162 cm

MATERIALS
Background fabric: 2 yards/2 metres
Contrasting prints for border and four-patch blocks: 1¾ yards/1.7 metres. This length allows for cutting the borders in a single piece. Small amounts of other fabrics which you already have may be used for the patchwork.
Backing: 2¾ yards/2.7 metres
Wadding: 52 x 68 in/132 x 173 cm

CUTTING

All measurements quoted include a standard ¼ in/0.75 cm seam allowance except where stated otherwise.

1 From the background fabric, cut 4 strips, each 8½ in/22 cm wide cutting across the full width. From these cut 17 squares, 8½ in/22 cm.

2 From the part-width remaining, cut 1 strip, 2½ in/6.5 cm wide and 1 strip, 1½ in/4 cm wide.

3 Cutting again across the full width cut 4 strips, each 4½ in/11.5 cm wide, 3 strips, each 2½ in/ 6.5 cm wide and 1 strip, 1½ in/4 cm wide.

4 Remove the selvage from the border fabric. Cutting lengthwise parallel to the selvages, cut 4 strips, each 4¾ in/12 cm wide.

5 From contrast fabric, for the pieced blocks, cut 4 strips, each 4½ x 9 in/11.5 x 23 cm, 9 strips, each 2½ x 10 in/6.5 x 26 cm and 5 strips, each 1½ x 12 in/4 x 32 cm.

SEWING

Piecing the blocks

The quilt contains three different blocks as illustrated (diagram 1): A, B and C.

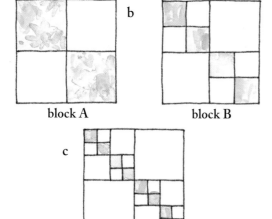

block A   block B

block C

Block A (make four)

1 Place a strip of background fabric, 4½ in/11.5 cm wide, right side up, then position a contrast strip of the same width on top, right sides together. Stitch, taking a ¼ in/0.75 cm seam, down one long edge and continue in this way with all the contrast strips (diagram 2). Press with the seams towards the prints. Note that there will be some background strip left over.

2 Measure carefully along the joined strip at right angles to the seam and cut off eight 'slices', each 4½ in/11.5 cm wide (diagram 3).

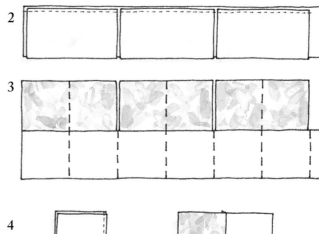

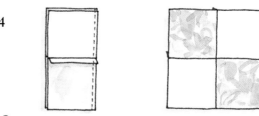

3 Place the slices with right sides together in pairs, with the contrast prints in opposite corners and stitch. Press the seams to one side (diagram 4).

Block B (make nine)

1 Use the same process to make smaller four-patch blocks, using the 2½ in/6.5 cm wide background strips and the matching contrast strips. This will make 18 small four-patch blocks, each 4½ in/11.5 cm square. Note again that this won't use all the background strip.

2 With right sides together, place each of the small blocks on a 4½ in/11.5 cm wide background strip and stitch (diagram 5). Cut across the background fabric between the attached four-patches to make 18 half-blocks (diagram 6). Place these together in pairs so that the contrast squares will form a diagonal line across the block and stitch. Check that you are sewing the seam correctly or the blocks will not come out right (diagram 7). Press.

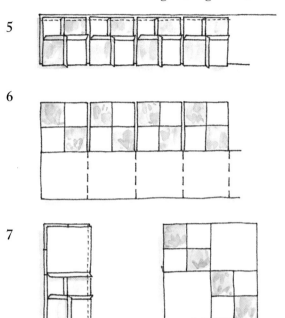

Block C (make five)

1 Use the same procedure as for block A to make 20 tiny four-patch blocks from the strips of background and contrast fabrics 1½ in/4 cm wide. These tiny blocks should measure 2½ in/6.5 cm square.

2 Repeat the process given in block B, step 2 above, to make 10 blocks, like smaller versions of block B, each 4½ in/11.5 cm square. Now repeat that process again to make five blocks, 8½ in/ 22 cm. Press.

PUTTING THE BLOCKS TOGETHER

1 When the blocks are ready, lay out the setting squares using the quilt plan (see page 138) as a guide. Fill in the spaces with the 18 pieced four-patch blocks, switching them about until you are satisfied with the arrangement, then stitch the blocks together in horizontal rows. Press the seams on alternate rows in opposite directions to help when matching the block seams at the next step.

2 Stitch the rows together, matching the block seams carefully and easing between as necessary.

ADDING THE BORDERS

1 Press under ½ in/1.5 cm on one long edge of each border strip. Stitch two border strips by their remaining unpressed edges to the two vertical sides of the quilt top.

2 Unfold the pressed-under edges and attach the other two borders to the top and bottom of the quilt. Press the ends of these strips in line with the existing pressed edges, trimming as appropriate. There should now be a pressed edge round all four sides of the quilt.

FINISHING THE QUILT

1 Divide the backing fabric in half and place it right sides together and selvages level. Stitch taking a ½ in/1.5 cm seam down one edge parallel to the selvages. Trim the selvages away before pressing the seam open.

2 Layer the backing, wadding and quilt together (see page 14) and baste or pin.

3 The original project was machine-quilted with a diagonal grid that could be marked with masking tape. The lines run through the corners of the squares. Position the tape carefully, so that one edge runs through the intended points, being sure to stitch beside the correct edge of the tape. The masking tape may be used for more than one line of sewing but do not leave it stuck to the fabric for any longer than necessary. After sewing a central line of quilting in one direction, sew a similar stabilising centre line in the other main direction of the grid. Gradually complete the grid, working outwards from these lines. Afterwards, quilt 'in-the-ditch' (see page 14) around the border.

4 Lay the quilt out on a flat surface and carefully trim the wadding, being careful not to catch the pressed edge of the border, to the same size as the quilt. Trim the backing to include ½ in/1.5 cm turning. Fold this to the inside over the edge of the wadding to enclose it and pin in place, level with the edge of the quilt. You may tack before machine-stitching through all layers to finish. Finally, sign or label the quilt.

THE CONTRIBUTORS

PAULINE ADAMS
Trained and worked as an architect, then as a town planner. She started as a quilter in 1957. A former member of The Quilters' Guild of Great Britain Executive Committee, she was one of the team operating the Guild's quilt documentation programme and contributed to the resulting book, 'Quilt Treasures' published in 1995. She is the author of a number of technical articles in 'The Quilter' magazine and of her own book on patchwork. She exhibits regularly at national and local shows.

Her particular interests are in patchwork techniques, especially in developing quick methods, and in lecturing.

COLIN BRANDI
Was introduced to patchwork quilts by an American quilter in 1989. Two years later he abandoned his career as an insurance broker to study for a degree in Art and Design. His current quilts explore issues of gender and he is developing his ideas on colour, pattern and form, working towards a one-man exhibition.

The majority of his work is constructed using rotary cutting, machine piecing and machine quilting techniques and his quilts have been displayed both at visual art exhibitions and quilt shows in the U.K. and Germany.

JENNI DOBSON
Studied art and textiles and is a qualified adult teacher. Her quilts have won rosettes at major British quilt shows, were selected by The Quilters' Guild for their fourth and fifth national exhibitions and have been displayed in America, Japan, Europe and Australia. She is a regular contributor to national patchwork magazines and has been teaching patchwork and quilting since the late 1970s. She has lectured and given demonstrations at major events in the U.K., Holland and Germany.

She is a keen quilter who loves to share her enthusiasm for the subject through teaching and writing.

GILL TURLEY
Studied art and fashion and began making quilts in 1982. She now works as a freelance speaker and teacher of quiltmaking. The Quilters' Guild selected her quilts to include in their national exhibitions in 1987, 1991 and 1993 and photographs of her quilts have featured in several recent quilt books. She has been a member of the Executive Committee of The Quilters' Guild since 1991 and currently holds the post of International Relations Officer.

She has been particularly influenced by the antique quilts and country fabrics which she has seen and admired on her travels.

ANNE WALKER
Trained as a mathematics teacher and has always had a great interest in geometric designs. She has been making quilts since the early 1980s, resulting in a career move to the teaching of patchwork and quilting. She is a prominent member of The Quilters' Guild, having been Education Officer and Vice President. She has been involved in setting up the curriculum for a national patchwork course and has written and contributed to other patchwork books.

She currently runs a patchwork and quilting supplies business, 'Piecemakers', where she aims to provide something special for the quiltmaker, including a very full range of workshops.

INDEX